Object-Oriented Software Metrics

B. MEYER
Eiffel: The Language
Object-Oriented Software Construction

D. MANDRIOLI AND B. MEYER (EDS.)
Advances in Object-Oriented Software Engineering

J.-M. NERSON AND B. MEYER
Object-Oriented Applications

D. COLEMAN ET AL.
Object-Oriented Development: The Fusion Method

B. HENDERSON-SELLERS
A Book of Object-Oriented Knowledge

H. KILOV AND J. ROSS
Information Modeling: An Object-Oriented Approach

M. LORENZ
Object-Oriented Software Development: A Practical Guide

M. LORENZ AND J. KIDD
Object-Oriented Software Metrics: A Practical Guide

P. J. ROBINSON
Hierarchical Object-Oriented Design

R. SWITZER
Eiffel: An Introduction

Object-Oriented Software Metrics
A Practical Guide

Mark Lorenz

Jeff Kidd

PTR Prentice Hall, Englewood Cliffs, New Jersey 07632

Library of Congress Cataloging-in-Publication Data

Lorenz, Mark
     Object-oriented software metrics : a practical guide / by Mark
Lorenz and Jeff Kidd.
       p.   cm.
     Includes index.
     ISBN 0-13-179292-X
     1. Object-oriented programming (Computer science) I. Kidd, Jeff.
II. Title.
QA76.64.L67 1994
005.1'4—dc20

94-5018
CIP

For Chammie . . . who always measures up.

Mark Lorenz

Dedicated to Alexander E. Watkins

Jeff Kidd

Editorial production: *bookworks*
Acquisitions editor: *Paul W. Becker*
Cover designer: *Aren Graphics*
Manufacturing manager: *Alexis R. Heydt*

© 1994 by P T R Prentice Hall
Prentice-Hall, Inc.
A Paramount Communications Company
Englewood Cliffs, New Jersey 07632

The publisher offers discounts on this book when ordered in bulk quantities. For more information contact: Corporate Sales Department, P T R Prentice Hall, 113 Sylvan Avenue, Englewood Cliffs, New Jersey 07632. Phone: (201) 592-2863, FAX: (201) 592-2249

Printed in the United States of America

10 9 8 7 6 5 4 3 2

ISBN 0-13-179292-X

Prentice-Hall International (UK) Limited, *London*
Prentice-Hall of Australia Pty. Limited, *Sydney*
Prentice-Hall Canada Inc., *Toronto*
Prentice-Hall Hispanoamericana, S.A., *Mexico*
Prentice-Hall of India Private Limited, *New Delhi*
Prentice-Hall of Japan, Inc., *Tokyo*
Simon & Schuster Asia Pte. Ltd., *Singapore*
Editora Prentice-Hall do Brasil, Ltda., *Rio de Janeiro*

Contents

DESIGN METRICS

33

Preface

This book identifies a key element in any software engineering effort: a set of meaningful metrics for measuring project progress and quality. These metrics apply specifically to object-oriented software projects. The metrics are based on measurements and advice derived from a number of actual projects that have successfully used object technology to deliver products. Five of these projects are individually detailed in the appendix.

I don't claim to have all the answers, but I do have practical advice to use today until someone has the "right" answer tomorrow. That's what this book is about: helping real development teams on OO projects estimate, schedule, and measure quality more effectively. As we learn more, I expect the metrics and anomaly thresholds and affecting factors to change. I view the state of OO metrics as a learning continuum—we will be better at it next year and the year after that. In the meantime, I have some information that has been useful on my OO projects that I am convinced will help you on yours too.

How to use this book

The intent of the metrics proposed in this book is to provide help for OO developers and managers to foster better designs, more reusable code, and better estimates. The metrics should be used to identify anomalies as well as to measure progress. The numbers are not meant to drive the design of the project's classes or methods, but rather to help us focus our efforts on potential areas of improvement.

I hope that I can promote the idea that these metrics are used on an ongoing basis by *developers* as well as technical leads and managers. I believe they can help each of us develop higher quality software systems and help us improve the way we develop that software. The metrics, as supported by tools, make us *think* about how we subclass, write methods, use collaboration, and so on.

My belief and goal are that *all* developers use and benefit from a continual periodic look at the metrics in this book. In fact, the majority of the metrics are design metrics! These are the easiest to automate and the most specific and prescriptive. I have found them useful in my efforts to estimate projects, measure progress, and review designs.

Who is this book for?

This is a practitioners' book to help people on ongoing OO projects develop software systems effectively. It is based on conclusions drawn from experiential data from a number of OO projects over the last few years. It is not grounded in mathematical proofs or theories. I welcome efforts to advance the industry in this area, but I don't want to wait until multiyear industry studies result in industry standards to provide help to practitioners. This book is for those who want to see the current results of a continuing work in progress.

The basis of this book

I originally began collecting OO metrics in late 1990, when I found that I had little to help me in my role as technical lead on a commercial development project with estimating or design reviews. I developed a tool and started collecting data from a number of Smalltalk and C++ projects at IBM as well as commercial products that included source code. In 1992, I worked on a second (better) iteration of a metrics tool and again collected (a different set of) metrics for a number of OO projects. In February 1993, I founded Hatteras Software and worked on a third iteration of a (better yet) metrics tool. This tool (which is in development toward product release while this book is being written) and the improved set of OO metrics support the results that appear in this book. During this time, an independent developer named Jeff Kidd worked under my direction on this tool.

This was an ongoing, evolving process and I collected different sets of metrics over the years. For example, I have sets of numbers to support estimating based on person-days per class but have project results that make me believe that person-days per public responsibility is a more accurate metric. So, I am collecting numbers to support this relatively newer metric and will begin using it as a basis for estimating as soon as I have calibrated it using commercial OO projects. I purposely choose to err on the side of measuring too much rather than too little.

Types of projects analyzed

I examined a set of C++ and Smalltalk projects containing from 60 to 700+ project-specific classes. The project durations were from 6 months to $2\frac{1}{2}$ years, with teams of 2 to 25 developers. Support personnel (test, management, and so on) added further to these numbers. The following chart shows the distribution of the sizes. Most of these are now commercial products; some are internal company tools. Most are Smalltalk implementations, at least partially due to the availability of the systems and tools. I have built three different versions of OO metrics tools. My latest will handle C++ code; the first two did not—I relied on other tools.

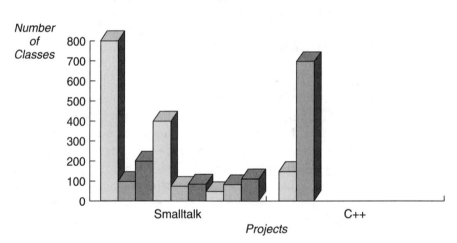

I have included some annotated individual product analyses in the appendix, with their histograms of key metrics shown and briefly discussed.

Methodology

I am a strong supporter of an extended responsibility driven design (RDD) type methodology, as defined in [WIRFS90], [JACOB92], and [LORENZ93]. This is certainly apparent in some of the metrics and advice in this book. However, I firmly believe that the vast majority of the information contained in this book applies across methodologies and languages, albeit with some adaptation in terminology and numbers. For example, [GIBSON90] *scenario scripts* are used here but can be correlated to [JACOB92] *use cases* .

What else is being done?

There is very little work to reference in the area of OO metrics in the industry. The most notable is the [CHID91] work at MIT. The biggest difference between this book and the MIT work is that this work draws from actual project experiences and iteration on the metric results. The MIT work is grounded in theory and evaluation criteria. The proposed metrics from the MIT work include

n Weighted methods per class

   The number of methods relates to the amount of effort to maintain the class and the reusability of the class.

n Depth of inheritance tree

   Nesting level relates to class complexity.

n Lack of cohesion in methods

   Grouping methods by references to instance variables may indicate the possibility of the need for additional class(es) along the lines of those groupings.

I participated in the OOPSLA '92 metrics workshop in Washington, D. C., where the current MIT work as well as the OO metrics work of others in the industry, such as Dr. Sallie Henry's, was presented. There were many issues and areas for further research identified but not a lot of conclusive progress.

Acknowledgments ———————————

I would like to thank all those who have helped make this book possible, especially those projects that allowed me to analyze their code.

I appreciate the efforts of the staff at Prentice Hall who did their magic on my manuscript. I'd like to thank my editor Paul Becker in particular.

I'd also like to thank the folks at Lotus, who developed a wonderful word processor named Ami Pro ™ that made this manuscript easier to write.

I would like to acknowledge the management of IBM's Object-Oriented Technology Center for allowing me to pursue object-oriented topics in depth.

Finally, I'd like to thank my family and co-workers, who have tolerated and supported my many hours of working on this book. In particular, I'd like to mention my wife Denise, daughter Kelly, and the people at Hatteras Software who I have had the privilege to work with including Bob Brodd, Bob Jensen, Ted Eiles, Tom Sarver, and Carol Jensen.

About the Authors

Mark Lorenz

Mark Lorenz is the founder and president of Hatteras Software, Inc., a company that specializes in helping projects use object technology successfully. He was formerly the technical lead of IBM's Object-Oriented Technology Center. He has been on multiple OO projects since 1987, mostly in technical lead roles, resulting in a number of products in different domains, including telephony, retail, banking, and insurance. Mark used structured techniques from 1977 to 1987.

Mark is the author of *Object-Oriented Software Development: A Practical Guide* (Prentice Hall, 1993). He has published articles in the *Journal of Object-Oriented Programming, The Smalltalk Report, Hotline on Object-Oriented Technology,* and *American Programmer* and participated on panels, tutorials, and workshops at conferences, including *ObjectWorld* and *OOPSLA.* He is a consultant on projects around the world to ensure their success in using object technology.

Mark welcomes comments and discussions via snail mail at

Hatteras Software, Inc.
208 Lochside Drive
Cary, N.C. 27511–9781

e-mail at 71214.3120@compuserve.com and voice mail or fax at 919.851.0993.

Jeff Kidd

Jeff Kidd was an associate programmer at IBM for a number of years. He supported Mark in his development of the third iteration of a tool to support collection of OO metrics. Jeff is currently self-employed.

Trademarks

HOMSuite and OOMetric are trademarks of Hatteras Software, Inc.

Smalltalk/V is a trademark of Digitalk, Inc.

OS/2 is a trademark of International Business Machines Corporation.

Profile/V is a trademark of First Class Software.

WindowBuilder is a trademark of ObjectShare, Inc.

Other product names mentioned throughout the book may be trademarks of their respective companies.

Callouts

Along the left margin of the pages of this book are *callouts*. Callouts are used to provide summarized text to enhance skimming sections as well as to emphasize key points. In addition, icons are used in the left margins to indicate areas of the book. Whenever you see a , a new group of related metrics is being identified and described in that section. Whenever you see a , a new metric is being identified and described in that section. Whenever you see a metrics icon with another icon overlaying one corner, such as , that means that the metric applies only in certain specific circumstances (the example above is used for metrics that apply only to languages that support multiple inheritance). Whenever you see a , two or more metrics are being used in combination. Whenever you see a , an item of interest is being highlighted for extra emphasis.

Introduction

Parts of the body were used for measuring . . .
The length of a joint in the thumb, called an inch.
A cubit was variously defined, based on the length of an arm.
. . . governments began to set standard measures.
The king's body would be used as a standard . . .
Kings changed from time to time.
Nations . . . began to measure length by standard measures
marked on metal bars.[1]

The metrics in this book are divided into two categories:

- Project

  These are used to predict project needs, such as staffing levels and total effort. They also measure the dynamic changes that have taken place in the state of the project, such as how much has been done and how much is left to do. These metrics are more global and less specific than the *design* metrics.

- Design

  These are measurements of the static state of the project design at a particular point in time. These metrics are more localized and prescriptive in nature. They look at the quality of the way the system is being built.

Within each of these categories, the metrics are further subdivided into logically related groups, such as method size and class internals.

---

[1] *The Volume Library* (The Southwestern Company, Nashville, TN, 1989), p. 1413.

For each metric, the following are listed and discussed:

- Name

  Each metric is given a unique descriptive name.

- Meaning

  A description of what is logically being discerned from a metric's measurements.

- Project results

  Graphs of statistics collected from actual OO projects are shown.

- Affecting factors

  In a number of cases, metrics are affected by factors that may not be readily apparent, such as the type of user interface (UI) used on the project. These factors are discussed on a metric-by-metric basis.

- Related metrics

  Metrics are listed in related groups, but there are a number of interrelationships that are useful. These are reflected in this section for each metric as well as a number of metrics listed as independent metrics of their own, which are based on combinations of metrics.

- Thresholds

  Thresholds are heuristic values used to set ranges of desirable and undesirable metric values for measured software. These thresholds are used to identify *anomalies,* which may or may not be an actual *problem.*

- Suggested actions

  Advice is given for action plans when metric thresholds indicate that a potential problem exists.

Appendixes include

- Project database
- Blank forms to collect metrics
- Related tools
- Future metrics

OO Software Metrics ─────────────────

A couple of points are worth making before getting into the specifics of individual OO metrics:

The metrics in the book are guidelines and not rules

■ The metrics are guidelines and not rules.

   While these metrics are based on actual project experiences, they are not "laws of nature." They are guidelines that give an indication of the progress that a project has made and the quality of the design.

■ The metrics should be used to support the desired motivations.

   The intent is to encourage more reuse through better use of abstractions and divisions of responsibilities, better designs through detection and correction of anomalies, and better estimates for development effort and schedules.

   It is not the intent to police or punish people on your team. Positive incentives, improved training and mentoring, and effective design reviews go hand in hand with the use of the metrics detailed in this book.

The metrics listed in this book are based on static snapshots of the system at a point in time. None of them are currently based on the runtime execution of the system. Any explicit or implied use of the word *dynamic* refers to the changes in state of the project measurements over multiple static snapshots.

Why are metrics important?

Deming's work on quality[2] has gotten a lot of attention in the United States in the last few years, largely because of the economic effects it has had in Japan. A key point of any attempt at improved quality, and its resultant increase in profits, is that we must *measure* where we are in our work. So, what do we measure, how do we interpret it once we have a measurement, and how do we relate the measurement to other efforts? That is what this book is about.

[2]"The Deming Prize: No Longer a Stranger at Home," *Computerworld* 23, no. 50 (December 11, 1989), p. 100.

■ Improved software quality

If we are to improve the OO software we develop, we must measure our designs by well-defined standards. Possible problems in our system designs can be detected during the development process.

[GILB85] suggests breaking down quality measures until reaching a set of directly measurable attributes. [KITCH92] uses this strategy to define measures for quality characteristics:

- Reliability
  Expected time to next failure

- Maintainability
  Average time to determine cause of a failure

- Extendibility
  Average productivity for code changes

- Usability
  Expected time to next nonfailure problem report

- Reusability
  Effort to create reusable components

You may consider these as quality measures if you don't have specific measures defined at your company.

■ Improved project management

If we are to estimate and manage our efforts, we must measure our progress effectively.

What's a Line of Code and Do We Care?

*A line of code is **not** a good measure of quality or progress and encourages larger volumes of code.*

Today's software metrics largely focus on an ill-suited measurement called a *line of code* (LOC). Using LOC as a metric has a number of drawbacks:

■ LOC is not consistent across languages, applications, or developers.

A LOC in assembly language provides far less end-user function than a LOC in Smalltalk or COBOL.

■ Code complexity is not reflected in LOC.

An intense graphical animation algorithm counts the same as code to set an array to zero.

■ LOC encourages larger code volume.

By measuring productivity based on LOC, we are rewarding programmers who write more code. What we want is *less* code with more function (such as through reuse)!

■ LOC is not a good predictor of quality or progress.

When we see a LOC measurement, we have not discovered anything about the reliability, performance, maintainability, or completeness of what we measured.

You will find LOC used in some of the discussions in this book. It is not emphasized, since it is not a good measure to base our work on, but it has some indirect benefits in other useful metrics. It is also still in great demand, largely due to the existing base of project statistics collected over the years.

Coding Style Effects and Normalized Methods

Smalltalk and C++ experiences show similar guidelines, with somewhat different thresholds.

The language used and different coding styles affect some of the metrics. This is primarily handled with different threshold values for the metrics which indicate heuristic ranges of better and worse values. For example, C++ tends to have larger method sizes than Smalltalk. The metrics in this book show threshold values for both C++ and Smalltalk in cases where the language used affects the numbers.

There are ways to minimize the affect of style issues. One such way is to standardize on measurements that are not affected by style, such as number of message sends in a method. Another way is to reformat the code to match a standard format.

About Thresholds

Thresholds are affected by many factors, including the state of the software (prototype, first release, third reuse, and so on) and your local project experiences. The thresholds given in this book reflect the experiences I have collected over a number of Smalltalk and C++ projects, but they are not absolute laws of nature. They are heuristics and should be treated as such.

Terms Used in This Book

There is a glossary at the back of this book that defines the terms used in this book. However, a few key definitions up-front will help with our discussions.

Metric

A standard of measurement. Used to judge the attributes of something being measured, such as quality or complexity, in an objective manner.

Measurement

The determination of the value of a metric for a particular object.

Design

That part of software development concerned with the mapping of a business model into an implementation.

Note that the terms used in this book are based on Smalltalk. Other terms are perfectly valid but are not used here for simplicity. For example, where I use *method* you can substitute *member function*.

Project Metrics

 This section contains a group of metrics that deal with the dynamics of a project. As a group, they are called *project metrics*. They deal with what it takes to get to a certain point in the development lifecycle and how to know that you're there.

These metrics can be used in a predictive manner, for example to estimate staffing requirements. They also can be used in an accounting fashion to measure progress toward the goal of completing the system development. In either case, unlike the *design metrics*, project metrics do not measure the quality of the software being developed. Being at a higher level of abstraction, they are less prescriptive and more fuzzy but are more important from an overall project perspective.

Project metrics overview

The table at the top of the following page lists the metrics that are covered in detail in this section of the book, showing interrelationships among the metrics.

Management Process

This book is not trying to define all aspects, techniques, or tools to use in managing or developing your software products. There are perfectly valid compatible techniques, such as using PERT charts, that I would encourage you to continue using in conjunction with the advice in this book.

Development Process

There have been a number of extensive discussions of what has been called an iterative, spiral, and incremental develop-

	N S S	N K C	N S C	N O S	P D C	C P D	N M I	N C C
Application Size								
Number of scenario scripts (NSS)	■							
Number of key classes (NKC)		■	◆					
Number of support classes (NSC)		◆	■					
Number of subsystems (NOS)				■				
Staffing Size								
Person-days per class (PDC)		◆			■		◆	
Classes per developer (CPD)					◆	■		
Scheduling								
Number of major iterations (NMI)							■	
Number of contracts completed (NCC)								■

Where: ◆ = cross-dependency between metrics exists

ment process, including [LORENZ93] and [BOEHM88]. A brief review of the process is needed as background information for this book.

I need to briefly touch on the terms *iteration* and *increment* as they relate to process. An iterative development process uses segments of time to develop multiple end-user functions. Some of these items will be new functions added for the first time (increments). Some of these items will be existing functions revisited for another time due to better understanding of requirements or quality concerns such as performance (iteration).

Iterative development process

The following diagram gives a high-level view of the iterative development process (IDP):

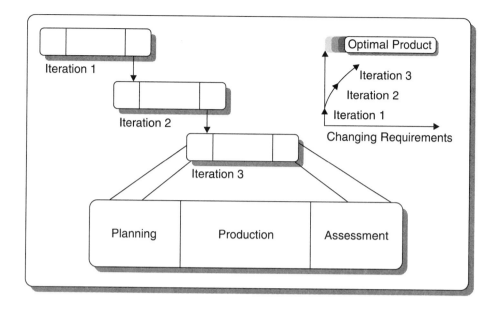

- Planning

  - Prioritize and update requirements
  - Schedule line items to develop during the *production* portion of the iteration
  - Document dependencies and deliverables

- Production

  - Work on line items scheduled during the *planning* portion of the iteration

- Assessment

  - Evaluate line items developed during the *production* portion of the iteration via customer reviews, design reviews, and driver usage

Development team

The diagram at the top of the following page depicts a suggested organization for your OO projects.

Note that the same person can play different roles at different times. It is not the intention that separate groups work on portions of the development and "throw the results over an organizational wall." In fact, I believe that the same person

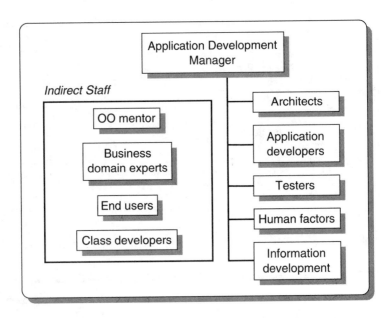

should be involved in the analysis, design, and implementation of a portion of the application.

- ■ Application development manager
  - Controls via OO metrics
  - Focuses on building products from reuse library components
  - Provides incentives for reuse
  - Allows time for iterations
- ■ Architects
  - Own the subsystem[3] contracts
  - Understand the key business classes
- ■ Business domain experts
  - Most knowledgeable about the industry (banking, retail, telephony, and so on)
  - Provide requirements clarification and terminology
- ■ OO mentors
  - Bring practical object technology experience to the project
  - Required for the paradigm shift

---

[3]A subsystem is a grouping of functionally related classes.

- "Grew" the core team, which seeds further in-house development
- Early defenders of the object model[4]

■ Class developers

- Designers and keepers of the most valuable software asset—the key model classes
- Work from the reuse library
- Application developers are their clients
- Growing set of people

■ Application developers

- Build applications from as many reuse library building blocks as possible
- Write a relatively small percentage (over time) of new code to specialize and complete the application
- Shrinking set of people

■ Support staff

- Iterate along with development
- Test organization—function tests the software based on scenario scripts
- Information development—writes on-line help and pieces of manuals as the system is being built
- Human factors—provides usability test results during the analysis phase

Application Size —————————————————————————

This section contains metrics used to measure the amount of work on a project, whether used for estimating future efforts or measuring completed line items.

Number of scenario scripts

Scenario scripts are written in certain OO methodologies[5] to document and leverage the expected uses of the system, as discussed in this section.

---

[4]The skill of developing a high-quality model of your business in objects takes time. Throughout the project, someone needs to resist the temptation to take shortcuts in model quality that provide tactical relief but strategic disaster.

[5]See [JACOB92], [LORENZ93], and [GIBSON90].

An example partial script for an inventory management system might look like the following:

Initiator	Action	Participant
User	requests Item information on	InventoryQueryWindow
InventoryQueryWindow	sends item: aNumber to	Inventory
Inventory	returns anItem to	InventoryQueryWindow
InventoryQueryWindow	requests price from	Item

• • •

Scenario script
A sequence of steps the user and system take to accomplish some task. Each step consists of an initiator, an action, and a participant.

A script is written for each major end-user function. The scripts have uses, such as inputs to test cases and the user manual, further downstream in the development lifecycle.

Meaning

The *number of scenario scripts* is an indication of the size of the application to be developed. Script steps should relate to the public responsibilities of the subsystems and classes to be developed. They also relate to the number of test cases to be written to fully exercise the system.

Project results

Being a relatively newer metric, I don't have much data to help with estimating. One data point I have is from a large C++ project I recently worked on that had 42 scripts and over 700 classes.

Affecting factors

■ Number of contracts

Contracts relate to public services (methods) available. Scripts should focus on exercising these public services. This is why scripts are key inputs to test cases and user manuals.

■ Number of requirements

Scenario scripts should directly relate to satisfying requirements. Scripts exercise major functionality of the system being built. The only reason this functionality should exist is to satisfy one or more requirements.

Related metrics

- Number of contracts

Thresholds

- There should be at least one script that exercises a subsystem contract, since these are the major functional requirements of the subsystem.

Suggested actions

- Low numbers, especially relative to the end-user functionality of the system, indicate that more scripts need to be written. There is no shortcut for this work—it requires that you get domain, object, and technical expertise in the same room and walk through scenarios of what the system does and how it's designed under the covers.

  These scenarios help fill in the details of the object model and provide inputs to the user manual and test cases.

Number of key classes

Key classes are central to the business domain being developed. They are typically discovered early in the analysis and thus give us something to leverage to get a handle on the amount of total work on a project. Key classes are also the central points of reuse on future projects, since they are highly likely to be needed in other domains in the business.

Key class
A class that is central to the business domain being automated. A key class is one that would cause great difficulties in developing and maintaining a system if it did not exist.

A key class can be related to a subset of an *entity* class in [JACOB92] or a *model* class in [BOOCH91]. If your methodology focuses more on UI and/or other types of classes, that is fine. This metric focuses on the underlying model classes that are central to your problem domain.

The *number of key classes* is a count of identified classes that are deemed to be of central importance to the business. While this is not a definitive judgment, you can usually determine if a class is key by asking questions such as,

Could I easily develop applications in this domain without this class?

Would a customer consider this object important?

Do many scenarios involve this class?

Answers to these questions will segregate classes into categories of key and support. Examples of key classes for some problem domains:

Retail	Telephony	Banking
SalesTransaction	*Call*	*SavingsAccount*
LineItem	*Connection*	*Currency*
Currency	*Switch*	*Customer*

Key classes facilitate early estimation of the amount of effort on a project.

Support classes usually include UI, communications, and database classes (obviously, if your application's purpose is in one of these areas such as communications, then these classes are key).

Meaning

Note

Key classes are an important long-term software asset of the business.

The number of key classes is an indicator of the volume of work needed in order to develop an application. It is also one indication of the amount of long-term reusable objects that will be developed as a part of this effort for applications dealing with the same or similar problem domain. This is due to the fact that these types of objects will be central to any application that exists in the same type of business and they will already exist in the company.[6] Since reusable components are more important and more difficult to develop, this number is especially important to the project.

Project results

- Results are discussed more fully in the section on *average number of support classes per key class.*

Affecting factors

- Type of user interface

  A more involved application UI will result in more of the system being made up of support classes to deal with the ap-

---

[6]It certainly does not guarantee that the components will be submitted to the company's reuse library, even though this should happen.

plication's interactions with the user via windows and dialogs.

Related metrics

- Number of support classes
- Average number of support classes per key class

Thresholds

- Thresholds for this metric are discussed more fully in the section on *average number of support classes per key class*. In general, project experiences have shown that you can expect 20–40 percent of your classes being categorized as key domain classes, with the rest being support (UI, communications, database, and so on) classes.

Suggested actions

- Low numbers of key classes (below 20 percent) may indicate that you need to explore more of your business domain to discover important abstractions to simulate your business. Examine your system requirements, looking for areas not covered by your current object model classes. Hold modeling meetings to expand your object model.

Number of support classes

Support class
A class that is not central to the business domain being automated but provides basic services or interface capabilities to the key classes.

A support class is a class that is not central to the business domain. In other words, you could conceivably develop the applications for the system without having this particular class. However, this class provides valuable functions that surround and support the *key* classes in the system.

Support classes include user interface classes. They also include base computer science classes, such as Collection, String, Stream, File, Database, and DDE. Finally, they include the numerous surrounding "helper" classes that come about as a natural part of developing a good OO design where classes frequently delegate to other self-managing, specialized classes.

Support classes are of interest because they give us a handle on estimating the size of the effort. Key classes are usually discovered early in the development process. If the number of support classes and/or a relationship to the number of key classes can be found, we will be able to plan and manage our projects better.

Meaning

The number of support classes is an indicator of the volume of work needed in order to develop an application. Support classes are discovered later in the development process.

Project results

■ Results are discussed more fully in the section on *average number of support classes per key class.*

Affecting factors

■ Type of user interface (UI)

UIs vary from none to direct-action graphical UIs (GUIs). This is the single most important factor in estimating the number of support classes, since the type of UI will have profound effects on the number of UI classes needed. Single document interface (SDI) and multiple document interface (MDI) UIs will both contain a number of windows and dialogs to support even a moderate size application.

Related metrics

■ Number of key classes

■ Person-days per class

Thresholds

■ I have found that the number of support classes varies between one and three times the number of key classes. The variance is primarily affected by the type of UI. GUIs tend toward two times as many classes in the final application; applications with no UI tend toward one times the number of classes. For example, if there are 100 key classes and a GUI is to be used, an early estimate might be for 300 total classes in the application.

Suggested actions

■ Lower numbers of support classes do not necessarily indicate any required action. As long as your requirements are being met, you should be fine as far as this metric is concerned.

- Higher numbers, taking other factors like type of UI into account, may indicate poor factoring into classes. It is desirable to have small, more independent classes, but this can be taken to the extreme. I know of one case, as told by my friend Jeff McKenna, where a consulting firm had gone into a railroad scheduling project and had identified thousands of objects (and they didn't even have a *Train* object!). Once Jeff worked with them, the number of classes dropped significantly (even with the addition of *Trains!*).

This is a fine area of distinction that is best handled through reviews with people having multiple years of OO project experience. If you don't have the expertise available, then look at the responsibilities of the classes and see if some of them naturally belong together, based on the kinds of objects they are. See if potential combinations simplify or convolute the design.

Average number of support classes per key class

Support classes are discovered as we go, often drawn out over the bulk of the project effort. Key classes, as we have discussed, are usually discovered early in the effort, during the initial object domain analysis iterations. The relationship between key and support classes is not a simple one, being affected by a number of factors including the complexity of the user interface.

This metric exists to try to find useful correlations between the two so that we can perform better estimating early in the project. Long term, this will require good record keeping on projects at your company. Short term, you can use the numbers we present here from our experiences as a starting point for your company's projects.

Meaning

The *average number of support classes per key class* metric indicates the total volume of classes that have resulted on a project. This metric can also be used to help estimate the total number of classes that will result on a project, based on previous projects' results.

Project results

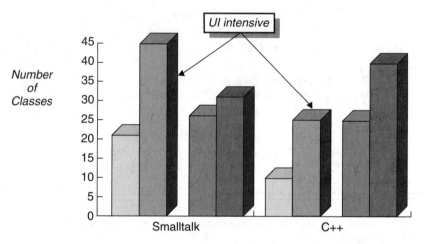

The graph shows a sampling of four projects. The first column of each pair shows the *key* classes and the second column of each pair shows the *support* classes for the same project. The results show

- UI intensive projects have **two to three times** as many support classes as key classes.

- Non-UI intensive projects have **one to two times** as many support classes as key classes.

These ratios give us ways to estimate the total number of classes in the final system. These ratios are estimates for the support classes only and must be added to the number of key classes.

Example

You find 100 key classes during the first weeks of analysis. You have a UI intensive project and use a ratio of 2.5, giving an estimate of 250 support classes. The total estimated number of classes for the final project is (100 + 250) or 350 classes.

Affecting factors

- User interface complexity

  The number of classes required to support a complex UI, such as a graphical user interface (GUI) under Presentation

Manager (PM) or Windows, will be greater than a simple interface.

■ Development team maturity

Less-experienced development teams (with less than a 1:6 ratio of OO experts to novices) will sometimes tend to create a plethora of model classes or very few model classes. This is due to factors such as creating new classes instead of reusing base classes, failing to recognize possible abstractions, and misunderstanding the intent of the OO concepts. Poor class selection will affect this metric.

Related metrics

■ Number of support classes

■ Number of key classes

Thresholds

■ Even for applications with no UI whatsoever, you should have at least as many support classes as you do key classes.

Suggested actions

■ A lower average may indicate that you are doing too much in too few classes. Take a look at the responsibilities in the classes and see if there are some natural groupings that can be divided into new classes. Think about the responsibilities, asking yourself:

Is there an entity in this domain which logically should take care of these responsibilities?

What would I call something that provided these services?

What other objects would this new entity work with?

■ Get OO expertise on your project to ensure good class selection and development. This is especially important during the early weeks of the object model analysis.

Number of subsystems

A subsystem is a collection of classes that support a set of end-user functions. Breaking the system up into relatively independent subsystems allows the project to divide up the work

Subsystem
A group of classes that work together to provide a related group of end-user functions.

among teams, much as in traditional development. The size of subsystems can vary greatly. The subsystems usually won't be discovered until after some amount of object domain analysis has been completed—they rarely match the subsystems found using traditional techniques.

A process for finding subsystems I have found successful looks like this:

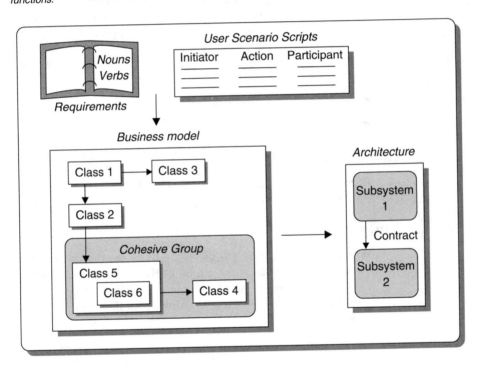

Our projects examine requirements documents, using parts of speech techniques. We write scenario scripts to discover the key classes and responsibilities in the business' object model. We then look for cohesive groupings of classes (subsystems) and responsibilities (contracts), creating an architecture that we can use to manage the development of large, complex systems.

Parts of speech

Candidate classes, subclasses, methods, and attributes are discovered by looking at nouns, verbs, and adjectives in requirements documents.

Scenario scripts

Time-ordered interactions between the user and system objects are written to help fill in details of the object model being constructed.

Develop an architecture

Classes that are more closely coupled, providing similar sets of end-user functionality, are grouped into logical entities called *subsystems*.

Major public services are logically grouped into sets of closely related protocols called *contracts*.

As long as the contracts that cross subsystem boundaries are managed for changes, different groups can develop the subsystems largely independently.

Examples of subsystems

Interface   Handles input and output, including reporting and mouse inputs

InventoryManagement
          Depletes and restocks items in inventory automatically

Meaning

The number of subsystems has an effect on scheduling possibilities, with each developed as a black box. The architecture between groups is controlled by controlling the interfaces to the subsystems. Subsystems also allow better documentation, since they are abstractions that help developers understand a large complex system.

Project results

■ Probably the most useful information about subsystems is the number of classes they contain. These numbers, based on individual preferences, vary greatly today.

Affecting factors

■ System size

The size of the system will affect the number of end-user functional groupings that are discovered. These groupings directly relate to the number of subsystems.

Related metrics

- Number of contracts
- Average number of classes per subsystem

Thresholds

- I would look for a minimal number of subsystems, perhaps three, as a lower threshold, since every system I have worked on has had at least that many subsystems. Instead of an upper threshold, I would look at the number of classes in any subsystem and the interfaces to them. If you can't describe a subsystem's high-level services or if it doesn't contain a number of closely related classes, then I would question the subsystem's purpose.

Suggested actions

- A subsystem is a grouping of classes, so take any subsystem that has only one or two classes and merge it into its containing subsystem.
- Reorganize loosely related classes into different groupings, based on the overall purpose (services) provided. Assign contracts to the subsystems, delegating them to classes within the subsystems.

An estimating example

In this section, I'd like to discuss an example of how I have estimated system size on previous OO projects. Be aware that some of the metrics used here are not as accurate as I'd like and that I am moving toward using different metrics in this area once I have enough data to support their use.

In this example, I use person-days per class for estimating. In the future, I plan to use person-days per public responsibility, which is at a more detailed level and therefore more accurate in predicting the amount of work to build a system. These will also be available relatively early in the analysis.

So, these are the best numbers we have today to help us in our efforts. Stay tuned for better numbers as we all learn more.

An estimating process

When I start working with a new OO project, I tell the technical leads and management to create their initial estimate using whatever means they have used in the past. This is the best starting point. For example, when I went to work on a large retail application, the initial estimate created this way and the estimates generated through the following steps ended up close enough to support the contention that plans can be built early and updated as we learn more. The steps:

1. Use analysis techniques, such as *parts of speech* and *scenario scripts* as defined above, to discover a majority of the key classes in your problem domain.

2. Categorize the type of user interface you have:

   - No UI   2.0
   - Simple, text-based UI   2.25
   - Graphical UI   2.5
   - Complex, drag-and-drop GUI   3.0

   These numbers come from examining the results, after the fact, from multiple OO projects to see how the type of UI affected the numbers and types of classes.

3. Multiply the number of key classes by the numbers from step 2. This is an early estimate of the total number of classes in the final system.

4. Multiply the total number of classes from step 3 by a number between 15 and 20 (person-days from the *person-days per class* metric), based on factors such as

   - the ratio of experienced to novice OO personnel, and
   - the number of reusable domain objects in the reuse library.

This is an estimate of the amount of effort to build the system.

A project estimating example

1. You use *parts of speech* techniques on your requirements document to discover the beginnings of an object model. You then write some *scenario scripts* for major services in your new system, filling in details in your classes and methods as

you go. After two weeks of object modeling, you end up with 100 key classes.

2. You decide you have a pretty typical graphical UI, so you use a multiplication factor of 2.5.

3. You develop an early estimate of the total number of classes in the system by multiplying the number of key classes by the number from step 2. Your early estimate of the number of support classes in the final system is (100 * 2.5), or 250 classes. Adding that to the key classes is (250 + 100) or 350 classes.

4. You know that you don't have any problem domain objects in your company's reuse library to reuse. You also know that you have a minimal amount of experienced OO people, at a 1:6 ratio. So, you decide to multiply the total number of classes from step 3 by 20. Your early estimate of the total amount of effort required to build the final system is (350 * 20), or 7000 person-days.

Staffing Size

Metrics in this category deal with staffing issues—How many people do we need? How long do we need them? and so on.

Average person-days per class

The average amount of effort spent on a single class is our best indicator of what amount of work will be required on a new project, once we have an estimate of the number of classes we will develop (see the *related metrics* section below).

Meaning

Scheduling, staffing, and funding a project will require an estimate of the amount of effort facing a project. The *average person-days per class* metric predicts this effort, leveraging the estimates of the number of key and support classes.

Project results

The following chart shows some actual numbers from OO projects. There are a number of potential reasons for the differences in Smalltalk versus C++ numbers, as detailed in the *affecting factors* section below. A couple of additional possible reasons are (speculation on my part):

- C++ developers may tend to develop larger classes.

- C++ is more cryptic and more difficult to reuse, resulting in more reinvention versus reuse.

- C++ developers may not make the transition to OO as well, since the hybrid language lets them write non-OO code.

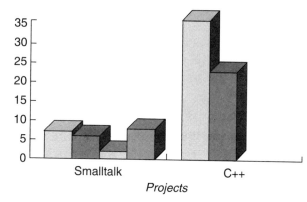

Average Number of Person-Days per Class

Projects

Affecting factors

Abstract class
A class which has no instances. A class which contains common methods and state data to facilitate sharing among its subclasses.

- UI versus model class

  UI classes have more methods and are more volatile than model classes.

- Abstract versus concrete class

  Abstract commonalities counterbalance the effort of subclasses. The more effort that can be gathered into abstract classes, the less effort the subclasses will require.

- Key versus support class

  Key classes normally will take more time to develop, since they embody the "essence" of the business domain, requiring more interactions with domain experts.

Concrete class
A class with instances in the runtime system.

- Framework versus framework client versus other

  Framework classes are powerful but are not easy to develop. You should expect to spend more effort on framework classes.

- Immature versus mature

  Mature classes typically have more methods but require less development time.

- Depth in inheritance hierarchy

  More deeply nested classes should take less effort to de-velop, since they should be specializations of the super-classes, generally with a fewer number of methods.

- Programming environment

  Integrated debuggers, class hierarchy browsers, incremental compilers, and other tools will speed up the development ef-fort.

- Class library

  The numbers, types, and maturities of classes available to reuse will greatly affect the productivity levels.

Related metrics

- Number of key classes

- Average number of support classes per key class

- Number of classes per developer

Thresholds

I use the following averages for my estimates. They are based on a number of projects I have been involved with over the last few years as well as any reported statistics I have been able to find in the industry.[7] As I stated before, I am moving to other bases for estimating, but this is the metric that I have the most data for today.

- Ten to fifteen days per production class

  Production class effort includes testing and documentation.

- Six to eight days to reach prototype level

  This includes development and unit testing (including some code to run tests) but not integration testing or formal test cases.

Suggested actions

- Use the higher estimate for your first project. Once you have experienced people in-house and you have off-the-shelf

Mature class
A class that has existed and been reused long enough so that it no longer changes very often.

Production class
A class which is fully developed and released in one or more com-mercial prod-ucts.

---

[7]For example, Tom Love quoted measurements from projects he worked with in a talk he gave at the ObjectWorld '91 conference.

classes that can be specialized, you can start estimating toward the lower end of the range of numbers. There are some assumptions for these numbers:

■ There is a 1:6 or higher ratio of OO experts to novices.

Higher ratios should result in lower average effort per class; lower ratios should result in higher average effort per class. This is because the productivity of the more experienced OO personnel will be higher than the novices. Also, the more experienced OO people will be able to mentor the novices, moving them along the learning curve faster.

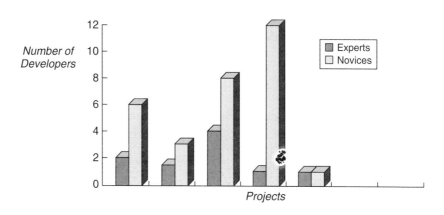

• There is no reuse library of components to reuse.

Components to use for specialization should result in lower average effort per class. If there are off-the-shelf components to reuse, there is less effort needed to build your application, since these components are already built, tested, and documented.

Average number of classes per developer

This metric leverages the number of key and support classes to estimate the number of staff needed on a project.

Meaning

The average number of classes per developer is useful to predict the number of developers needed on a project.

Project results

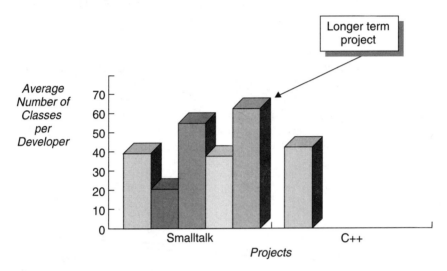

Over time, developers can own more classes, since the earlier classes have quiesced as they matured.

Affecting factors

■ Active versus maintained classes

There is a significant difference in the number of classes being actively developed versus the number of classes being maintained that a developer can be expected to own. The normal lifecycle of a class moves it from time-intensive development iterations, to less time-intensive "firming up" during subsequent work on the next one to two projects, to low effort maintenance of a solid, reusable class.

■ Skill level of the personnel

Skilled OO developers can own more classes than novices.

■ Subsystem class groupings

It typically makes sense for teams to follow cohesive groupings of classes into subsystems. This may tend to cause developers to own more or fewer classes than they would otherwise own.

Related metrics

■ Person-days per class

Thresholds

People on shorter projects (under 18 months) typically will "own" fewer classes than people on longer projects. The biggest reason for this fact is that, over time, changes to classes quiesce. It is relatively easier to own many stable classes than it is to own fewer classes being actively developed. Here are the rules of thumb I use, based on observed numbers from OO projects I have examined:

- Short-term project

  - Twenty classes per developer

- Long-term project

  - Forty classes per developer

Suggested actions

- Assign your key classes to your best OO developers. Watch levels of reuse and number of reported problems to determine who needs help with the classes they already own. Add classes to people's workload as class efforts, including support for function testing, have ended for previously owned classes.

An example

You have done an early analysis and discovered fifty key classes. You have estimated a total of 200 classes for your application. You have a mix of experienced and novice OO developers for a relatively short-term project (under one year). You decide to assign subsystems to your most experienced people who were involved in the analysis effort. They will own the key classes in each of their subsystems and will assign other class development to the novice developers. You estimate that your experienced developers will eventually own forty classes each and your novice developers will eventually own twenty classes each. You start with a staff of three experienced developers and add four more people over the first few weeks of the project. Originally, each developer is actively developing the first few classes they own, adding groups of classes as classes move into function testing.

Scheduling

This set of metrics deal with project scheduling: What was done on the last iteration? How many iterations have we done? How many iterations can we expect to do? and so on.

Number of major iterations

A major iteration is a multimonth effort on a number of line items.[8] I am assuming a project of significant size and not an extremely small task. The number of iterations has an effect on the product release schedule possibilities.

Iteration
A single cycle of an iterative process, consisting of planning, production, and assessment phases over a multimonth period of time.

Meaning

Iterating on software under development is almost required to "get it right." High-quality software in this world of changing and complex requirements is very difficult to develop without multiple efforts on portions of the product. Iterations allow early validation of our efforts.

Project results

Iterative process
Development steps that result in multiple deliveries of the same application functions over the life of the project.

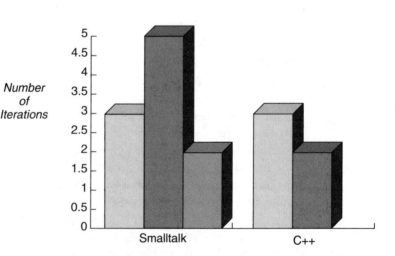

[8]See Mark Lorenz, *Object-Oriented Software Development: A Practical Guide* (Englewood Cliffs, NJ: Prentice Hall, 1993) for a complete discussion of the iterative development process (IDP).

Affecting factors

■ Support organization processes

The way in which your support organizations, such as test and information development, work will affect the way you will want to set up your iterations. These organizations should iterate with you. If they don't, you need to adapt to facilitate their efforts in conjunction with your iterations.

■ End-user availability

A big part of the benefit of using iterations is to get user feed-back, such as requirements clarification. End-user availability will therefore affect your iteration schedule.

Related metrics

■ None.

Thresholds

■ Three to six major iterations tend to work best.

Fewer iterations are probably not enough to get the desired benefits from the *assessment* portion of the iteration. More iterations will drag out the time between releases.

Suggested actions

■ Iterations tend to result in firmer requirements, better designs, and more usable systems. Try to stay within a range of three to six major iterations, each 2.5 to 4 months long. Within the *production* portion of the iteration, you will certainly be developing and delivering portions of the system as line items are worked on.

Number of contracts completed

Completion of the major architected public service interfaces to the system is the best overall indicator of project completion status I know of today.

Meaning

Contracts make up the public service protocols of the system under development. They are a good means to measure progress in delivering end-user functionality.

Project results

Contract
*A simplifying
abstraction
of a group of
related public
responsibili-
ties that are
to be pro-
vided by sub-
systems and
classes to
their clients.*

■ This is the direction I am pursuing for future estimating, since I believe it will be more accurate than class-based estimates. Estimating effort and completion status based on delivered contracts alleviates the inconsistencies I've encountered using delivered classes:

- Subclasses
  –Subclasses generally take less effort to develop, since
  –they are specializations of their superclasses.
- UI versus model classes
  UI classes are more volatile than model classes.

Affecting factors

■ None.

Related metrics

■ None.

Thresholds

■ There should always be some contracts being completed during any scheduled iteration. Certainly, an anomaly threshold is above zero. I would gear the anomaly level according to the necessary progress to meet my schedule deadlines.

Suggested actions

■ Hold design reviews for those contracts that are behind schedule, and create an action plan to make better progress.

An example

You work through a few weeks of domain analysis, developing a set of key classes and a few subsystem groupings. As you went, you discovered 100 contracts, shared among the classes and subsystems. You decide to use contract completion as one measure of project progress. Upon completion of the first major project iteration, you find that five contracts are completely developed, with a resulting status of 5 percent progress toward project completion.

Design Metrics

This section contains a group of metrics that deal with the static characteristics of a design. As a group, they are called *design metrics*. They take a look at the quality of the project's design at a particular point in the development cycle. Design metrics tend to be more locally focused and more specific, thereby allowing them to be used effectively to directly examine and improve the quality of the product components.

I really believe that metrics shouldn't be the job of one person, who runs them once a month to feed numbers into a management status meeting. These metrics can really have a positive day-to-day effect on each of the developers' designs. They require easy-to-use tools to support more frequent metric analyses. When given the tools, I hope that projects will start fostering the attitude that this is not a "bean counter" job but rather a useful job to help us *engineer* our software more effectively.

Design Metrics Overview

The table on the following pages summarizes the interdependencies of the design metrics.

Method Size

A method's size can be measured in a number of different ways. These metrics are grouped in this section and deal with quantifying an individual method.

Number of message sends

The *number of message sends* metric measures the number of messages sent in the method, segregated by type of message. The types include:

	N O M	L O C	M C X	S M S	P I M	N I M	N I V	N C M	N C V	H N L	M U I	N M O	N M I	N M A	S I X	C U A	G V X	I O S	P F U	F P M	F O U	C L C	P C M	P R M	C R C	N C T
Method Size																										
Number of message sends (NOM)		◆																								
Lines of code (LOC)	◆																									
Method Internals																										
Method complexity (MCX)	◆	◆																								
Strings of message sends (SMS)																										
Class Size																										
Number of public instance methods (PIM)						◆																				
Number of instance methods (NIM)					◆		◆																			
Number of instance variables (NIV)						◆																				
Number of class methods (NCM)									◆																	
Number of class variables (NCV)								◆																		
Class Inheritance																										
Hierarchy nesting level (HNL)											◆	◆	◆													
Multiple inheritance (MUI)																										
Method Inheritance																										
Number of methods overridden (NMO)										◆																
Number of methods inherited (NMI)										◆																
Number of methods added (NMA)										◆																
Specialization index (SIX)										◆																

Where: ◆   = cross-metric dependency exists

	N O M	L O C	M C X	S M S	P I M	N I M	N I V	N C M	H C V	M N L	N U I	N M O	N M I	S M A	C I X	G C O	I U S	P V U	F P M	F F U	C O C	P L M	P C M	C R C	C R P	N C T
Class Internals																										
Class cohesion (CCO)																▓	◆									
Global usage (GUS)																	▓									
Instance variable usage (IVU)															◆	▓										
Parameters per method (PPM)																		▓								
Friend functions (FFU)																				▓						
Function-oriented code (FOC)																				▓						
Comment lines per method (CLM)																						▓	◆			
Percentages of commented methods (PCM)																						◆	▓			
Problem reports per class (PRC)																								▓		
Class Externals																										
Class coupling (CCP)																									▓	
Class reuse (CRE)																									▓	
Number of classes thrown away (NCT)																										▓

Where:　◆　　= cross-metric dependency exists

- **Unary**

  These are messages with no arguments.

- **Binary**

  These are messages with one argument, separated by a special selector name. Examples are string concatenation and math functions.

- **Keyword**

  These are messages with one or more arguments.

Meaning

This measurement quantifies the size of the method in a relatively unbiased way. Other means of measurement, such as
LOC, do not take into account factors such as coding style
when measuring method size.

The following diagram shows two pieces of Smalltalk
code that provide exactly the same function but do so with a
different coding style. If we were to compare the pieces of code
based on physical lines of code, we would end up with twice
as many lines in the first case. Counting message sends more
accurately compares the two. "Normalizing" the methods,
such as by formatting them the same, would also help remove
style differences.

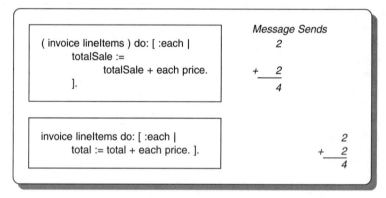

Project results

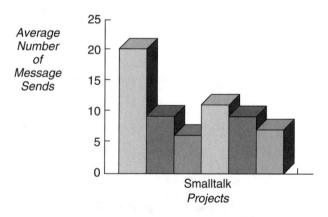

$$\frac{\text{total number of message sends}}{\text{total number of methods}}$$

Affecting factors

■ Language

Coding in a hybrid language, such as C++, allows the developer to write code in methods that are outside the "OO part" of the language. This code will not, of course, be counted in the number of message sends but certainly relates to the size of the method. We wouldn't want to ignore 100 lines of non-OO code and count a couple of message sends (member function invocations).

Related metrics

■ Lines of code

A good example of style effects is evident when you have a method that has a relatively high number of lines of code but an acceptable number of message sends. This is a sure indication that coding style has skewed the lines of code results.

■ Number of compiled bytes

The efficiency of a compiler should not affect the "standard" comparison of the size of an application.

Thresholds

■ I use nine for an upper anomaly threshold. Large numbers may indicate function-oriented code and/or poor allocation of responsibilities.

Suggested actions

■ Provide mentoring for developers who are writing larger methods. They are probably falling back on old habits and writing their methods in a more serial, function-oriented fashion instead of requesting services from other objects. Larger numbers of smaller classes are, in general, better.

Number of statements

What constitutes a statement depends on the language.

Smalltalk

We use an *expressionSeries* as defined by the Smalltalk BNF grammar in [DIGI89] as a statement for this metric. Examples of statements are

> ^account balance printString
> answer := ItemDialog new open choice.

C++

A statement in C++ as defined in [STROU87] is the same as a statement for this metric. Examples are

> day = d ? d : today.day;
> sw = point(a.x,b.y);

Meaning

The *number of statements* metric measures the size of method code in a less biased manner.

Let's look at the same piece of code from the *number of message sends* metric:

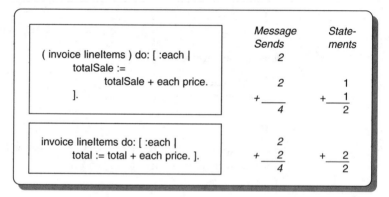

Project results

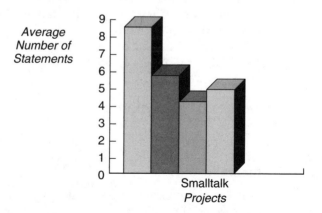

$$\frac{\text{total number of statements}}{\text{total number of methods}}$$

Affecting factors

- Language

  The definition of what constitutes a statement in the language will obviously affect this metric.

Related metrics

- Number of message sends
- Lines of code

Thresholds

- The trend is for this metric to run at about 80 percent of the level of the *number of message sends.* So, I multiply 0.8 times the threshold I use for *number of message sends.*

Suggested actions

- Provide mentoring for developers who are writing larger methods. They are probably falling back on old habits and writing their methods in a more serial, function-oriented fashion instead of requesting services from other objects. Larger numbers of smaller classes are, in general, better.

Lines of code

Meaning

The *lines of code* metric measures the number of physical lines of active code that are in a method.

Measuring lines of code is a relatively biased measure of method size which does not take coding style into account.

This measurement quantifies the size of the method without taking into account factors such as coding style when measuring method size. The way that a developer chooses to indent lines, go to a new line, and use long variable names will affect this measurement. This metric is included due to the continued desire on the part of projects to view these numbers and due to the fact that a great deal of project data is available on this metric.

Project results

The averages from measured projects are shown in the section on *average method size.*

Affecting factors

■ Developer style

The following example, taken from Smalltalk/V, shows how much style can affect LOC counts. You can get results that are two times the same code with a different style.

```
OrderedCollection>>copyFrom: beginning to: end
    "Answer an OrderedCollection containing the
    elements of the receiver from index position
    beginning through index position end."
| answer |
(answer := self species new: self size )
    startPosition: 1
    endPosition: end - beginning + 1.
^answer
    replaceFrom: 1
    to: end - beginning + 1          One keyword message
    with: self
    startingAt: beginning
```

The style choice (for readability) of breaking up the parts of a keyword message onto different physical lines drives the LOC count up. This would not happen with *number of statements* or *number of message sends* measurements.

■ Language

Different languages provide different functionality for the same physical code space (e.g., the functionality in a LOC of assembler is not equal to a LOC of Smalltalk).

Related metrics

■ Number of message sends

Thresholds

For Smalltalk projects, I recommend a threshold of six lines of code, *on average,* for methods. Smaller is generally better.

For C++ projects, I recommend a threshold of 24 lines of code, *on average,* for methods.

Of course, what I really (highly) recommend is that you don't use LOC at all!

Suggested actions

■ Review code for classes with large methods overall.

Don't bother with UI classes' *open* methods or accessing methods. Watch for function-oriented code. Make sure that a focus on reuse through collaboration and inheritance exists. Provide additional mentoring for anyone who is having trouble developing good OO designs.

Average method size

Across your project, your methods should on average be small. By looking across a number of methods, you can get a feel for the overall project's design quality.

Meaning

Note

The size of methods is a good indicator of the quality of your OO design. Methods should be short, on average.

The *average method size* is one indication of the quality of the design from an object perspective. Larger numbers indicate a higher likelihood that function-oriented code is being written. Smaller numbers indicate a higher likelihood that object-oriented code is being written. A growing average method size is another indicator that the design is not as good as it could be.

It is not a certainty but rather an anomaly worth investigating. There are large methods that are perfectly fine, as has been discussed elsewhere in this book. It is much more certain that a large average method size is a problem.

Project results

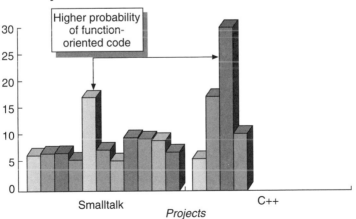

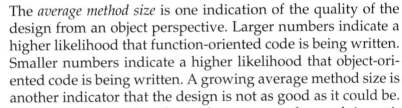

$$\frac{\text{total lines of code}}{\text{total number of methods}}$$

I've included lines of code in this section because the largest number of measured projects' results is based on lines of code. Once I have more data points for other metrics, I will no longer carry LOC in this section.

The following graph shows fewer data points but for a better metric: *number of message sends.*

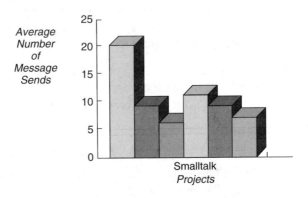

total number of message sends
---
total number of methods

Affecting factors

■ Key classes

Classes at the center of your application will often be larger and more complex.

■ UI classes

User interface classes will have some large methods, such as the initial layout of the window contents. This may skew your averages higher.

■ Active versus passive classes

Classes that take an active role in driving the behavior of the system will generally be larger and more complex than passive, data-providing objects.

■ Accessing methods

Methods that allow access to state data in classes are typically very short. This will skew your averages lower.

■ Language

C++ method sizes tend to run higher than Smalltalk. I use a higher threshold for C++ projects to identify anomalies.

Related metrics

- Number of message sends
- Lines of code

Thresholds

My experience over the last few years has been that the *average method size* for Smalltalk should be under six lines of code. I hate to use LOC, but that is the metric for which I have the largest number of measurements from actual projects. For C++, I use 18 as the threshold value.

I have fewer measured project results to support this number, but I use nine message sends per method as my threshold average. This number applies to both Smalltalk and C++.

Suggested actions

Hold design reviews to examine the contents of the methods, especially in areas that are on average larger and/or growing in size.

Be aware that UI classes will have some large methods, such as a method to create a particular window layout. This is not a problem and should be offset by using an average across a number of classes and methods as a telltale for quality problems or by excluding layout methods entirely.

An example

You perform a metrics analysis on your code, as you do every couple of weeks to aid in developing good designs. You discover, to your amazement, that one of your model classes has swollen to over 80 methods. The rest of your model classes have under 20 methods each. Your UI classes are running over 40 methods, but you know that you are using a complex GUI interface and don't worry about that.

You look more closely at the 80+ method class. In thinking about it, you discover that there are two main groupings of responsibilities. In discussing it with another person on the project, you decide that there is another type of object in the system that you hadn't realized was there before you started prototyping the system.

You create another class, moving methods from the 80-method class based on relationships to the responsibility groupings. You initially end up with two classes with 45 and 35 methods in them. You then find that, as you clean up the design changes, some methods go away and some methods are shortened by the changes. While the two classes are still larger than you'd like, your understanding of the application domain and the quality of the design has improved, while the code volume has actually decreased!

This may sound like fiction (which it is!), but this type of scenario happens time and again on OO projects. I encourage you to rework (iterate) sections of the system.

Method Internals

This group of metrics deal with the internal characteristics of the classes' methods.

Method complexity

There has historically been a lot of work done in the area of code complexity, including [MCCABE76] and [DREGER89]. Most of this work focuses on factors such as number of decision points made in the code of a function, surfaced in IF-THEN-ELSE and other constructs. There are basic differences in what OO code looks like that make these measurements less useful:

- Short methods

    Traditional complexity measures do not take into account the differences in OO designs.

    Function-oriented systems typically have a page of code. OO methods typically have less than six lines! There are many more, smaller components. Numbers in an experience database from function-oriented projects will not be directly comparable to OO project results.

- No case statements

    Well-designed OO systems don't use case statements.[9] In fact, Smalltalk doesn't even have a case statement! This further skews OO versus traditional system complexity measurements.

[9]It is true that something akin to a case statement lookup (even though it might be via a dictionary) is often used on the boundaries to OO systems, but the internals of the OO system shouldn't need case statements.

Object-oriented example	Function-oriented example

```
( accounts ) do: [ :eachAccount |
    eachAccount printTo: aFile.
].
```

```
for ( i=0; i < numAccts; i++ )
    switch ( accounts[i].type ) {
        case 1 :
            printSavings( accts[i] );
            break;
        case 2 :
            printChecking( accts[i] );
            break;
        ...
    }
```

■ Fewer IF statements

The use of inheritance to have single-minded self-managing objects leads to less checking of types of objects to decide what actions to take. A *CDAccount* doesn't need to check to see if it should incur a penalty upon withdrawal—it is designed to work that way, just as a *SavingsAccount* is built without any penalty behavior. This results in *fewer* conditional structures, again skewing the numbers compared to function-oriented code.

Good OO designs will make the historical measurements of complexity less useful. Other measurements that have meaning for OO code are needed, at a minimum as supplements to the traditional measures.

It is proposed that a complexity measurement that looks at the number and types of message sends in a method be the basic measurement of complexity.

Meaning

We are using the following assigned weights to compute method complexity:

■ API calls   5.0

■ Assignments   0.5

■ Binary expressions   2.0
  (Smalltalk)
  or arithmetic operators (C++)

- Keyword messages   3.0
  (Smalltalk) or messages
  with parameters (C++)

- Nested expressions   0.5

- Parameters   0.3

- Primitive calls   7.0

- Temporary variables   0.5

- Unary expressions   1.0
  (Smalltalk) or messages
  without parameters (C++)

There is no magic to these numbers. They were assigned values and are meaningful in relation to each other. Any good tool should let you adapt weights to your situation.

Project results

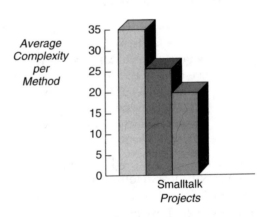

$$\frac{\text{total number of complexities}}{\text{total number of methods}}$$

Affecting factors

- Type of UI

  Methods to deal with complex windows will tend to be more complex. An example is a method to enable and disable menus based on the current state of the window and the system.

Related metrics

- Halstead metrics

- McCabe metrics

  I don't discuss these more traditional complexity metrics in this book. They are listed as a matter of reference for those who wish to look at the numbers collected from function-oriented projects over the years. They will need to be recalibrated to OO systems to be effective.

Thresholds

We use a threshold of 65 for our complexity measure. It is derived from evaluating a number of projects over the last few years and judging, based on our experience, which complexities should be considered a good anomaly threshold. Obviously, not a scientifically based foundation but in keeping with my focus on practical useful information until the "right" answer is found.

Suggested actions

Some complex methods are to be expected. I suppose you could keep taking the OO paradigm down to the level where nothing would be very complex. My experience has been that you end up with some situations where it makes sense to leave some amount of functionality together, even if a method is more complex than you'd like.

Some observed cases:

- Output formatting methods

  These methods are complex only because of the amount of stream manipulation, string concatenation, and other activities taking place across a number of objects. This could be distributed across the objects, but you may not want this mess in all your objects.

- Changes in key class relationships

  When you are changing some relationships between key classes, you potentially have a fair amount of work to do to clean up the system. This most often occurs at the "center" of your application.

- UI methods

  We have often talked about *open* methods, which construct potentially complicated GUI views. Another example is an *updateMenu* method, which handles the enabling and disabling of menus based on object selections and other menu actions.

For cases other than those listed above (and additional exceptions which you judge to be valid), you will want to try leveraging other objects' capabilities and the same object's
capabilities through message requests. Try to end up with one
basic client function being provided by one method.

Strings of message sends

In Smalltalk, messages can be strung together. This helps in
coding in a style that approaches the problem domain language, such as *myAccount balance print*. However, there are implications for error recovery when methods are implemented
with multiple messages strung together, feeding the next message down the pike with an intermediate object from the last
message send.

   A candidate metric is to relate strings of message sends
to error recovery indicators as a design measurement.

Meaning

Stringing messages together decreases the amount of intelli-
gent error handling that can be performed. For example, intermediate object results are shown for the following code:

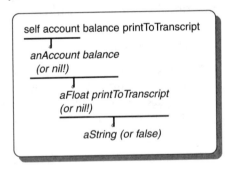

What happens if *self account* returns *nil* instead of *anAccount?*
A runtime error occurs. This particular possibility could be
handled a number of ways, including laissez-faire initialization. For example, I might code the *account* accessing method
as follows:

```
account
    ( Account isNil) ifTrue: [ account := Account new. ].
    ^account
```

Therefore, I know I cannot get a *nil* object back at this point, although returning a new *Account* object may not be a valid action at this point either!

Similarly, the account's balance may be *nil*. Again, a self-initializing strategy can be followed, which probably makes sense in this case. But, what if the balance comes back as an *Integer* instead of a *Float?* Maybe this matters; maybe it's fine.

What if the *printToTranscript* method expects *aString* instead of *aFloat?* This could be handled by inserting *aString* as another message before calling *printToTranscript*.

The point is not that error handling can't be dealt with; it's that the issue exists at all. Well-designed systems can, in general, do a good job of error detection and recovery (see [HINK93] and [CHRI93]). This metric looks at the lengths of strings of message sends. I don't claim to understand at this point how useful looking at this measurement will be. I discuss this metric in order to err on the side of collecting too much, rather than collecting too little.

Project results

Unfortunately, I don't have measurements from the projects I've been involved in for this metric. Work has been done in the different languages and environments to partially alleviate the concerns detailed in this section.

Affecting factors

■ Environment exception handlers

Some exceptions are handled by the environment or by general-purpose exception handlers. Identify those key areas of your system that are not adequately covered by these facilities and write your code so that you can detect and handle error situations yourself.

Objectworks/Smalltalk™ by ParcPlace has exception handling capabilities built into the base class hierarchy.

C++ has *try/throw/catch* capabilities (see [MEYERS92]) to handle errors.

Related metrics

■ Number of message sends

Thresholds

None set at this time.

Suggested actions

Include your error-handling schemes in your considerations of how you design the system. For example, if in Smalltalk capturing *doesNotUnderstand* and logging the problem along with laissez-faire initialization in accessing methods are not good enough, then you may need to look at how you are stringing your messages together. In particular, you may want to check the type of object returned or have your methods return *nil* when errors occur, so that clients can easily detect the error.

Class Size

A class' size can be measured in a number of different ways. These metrics are grouped in this section and deal with quantifying an individual class.

Number of public instance methods in a class

Public methods are those that are available as services to other classes. These services are the best way to judge the amount of work being done by a class. In contrast, *private* and *protected* methods are those the class uses to get its work done to honor the public services it has made available.

Meaning

Public methods are an indicator of the amount of work being done in a class, since they are the services being used by other classes.

The *number of public instance methods in a class* is a good measure of the amount of responsibility in the class. The public methods comprise the contracts tested during verification and drive the work done in the class.

Project results

I have not been collecting numbers on public methods separately from instance methods in general. See the *number of instance methods in a class* metric for project results. Public methods will most effectively help in the estimating process.

Affecting factors

■ Passive "data" objects

Informational objects that take a passive role in the system, existing to provide information when queried, often consist largely of public accessing methods and have fewer service-oriented protocols.

■ Superclasses

The inherited public methods from the superclasses are available as services from this class. Perhaps the public methods defined in this class should be looked at separately from inherited methods, as well as together.

Related metrics

■ Class hierarchy nesting level

Classes farther down the hierarchy should generally have fewer methods, and thus fewer public methods. Counting all the methods available up the hierarchy, the nested classes will have more public methods on average.

Thresholds

The total number of instance methods threshold I use is 20, so this number is below that on average. Since it is not easy to detect this metric for Smalltalk, I don't have good numbers from Smalltalk projects. For C++, these methods are in the *public* section, of course, and are therefore detectable by tools.

Suggested actions

Use the number of public methods to help in estimating the amount of work to develop a class or subsystem.

Number of instance methods in a class

The total *number of instance methods in a class* counts all the public, protected, and private methods defined for a class' instances.

Meaning

The number of methods in a class relates to the amount of collaboration being used. Larger classes may be trying to do too much of the work themselves instead of putting the responsibilities where they belong. They are more complex and harder to maintain.

Smaller classes tend to be more reusable, since they provide one set of cohesive services instead of a mixed set of capabilities.

Project results

The results for the measured projects are in the section on the *average number of instance methods per class*.

Affecting factors

- Depth in the inheritance hierarchy

  Classes farther down in the hierarchy should have fewer instance methods, since they should be specializing existing superclass(es).

- Class maturity

  Mature classes can have higher numbers. Over time, new requirements will typically add new instance methods.

Related metrics

- Number of class methods

- Number of instance variables

Thresholds

I use an upper threshold of 20 for the number of instance methods in a model class. I use 40 for UI classes.

Suggested actions

Look for missing classes. Examine patterns of instance variable usage to see if there are useful ways to split the class. Make sure responsibilities don't belong with other classes.

Average number of instance methods per class

Too many methods in a single class (not counting inherited methods) are a warning sign that too much responsibility is being placed in one type of object. This metric should focus on the *public* methods, since these are the responsibilities that relate to the amount of work the class is signed up to do. The private methods are merely the way in which the class is designed to do its work to fulfill the public method contracts.

Meaning

The number of instance methods in a class correlates to the amount of responsibility handled by the class. Good OO designs distribute intelligence and workload among many cooperating objects.

Project results

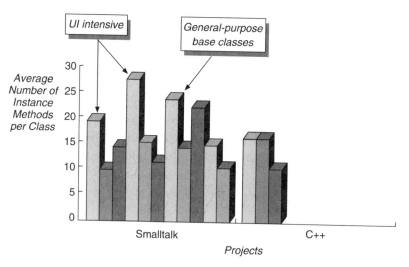

$$\frac{\text{total number of instance methods}}{\text{total number of methods}}$$

Affecting factors

- ■ UI classes

  User interface classes will have a larger number of methods, since they must service each of the controls and menu actions on the screen. A large number of methods in a UI class is probably not an indication of a quality problem.

- ■ Mature classes

  As classes mature, they will tend to increase in size as new requirements are placed on them.

Related metrics

- ■ Instance variable usage

Thresholds

- ■ Twelve as an average for model classes; 25 as an average for UI classes. The thresholds for averages should be lower than for individual anomalies.

Suggested actions

■ Design reviews

Hold design reviews to examine the class to see if some of the methods don't make sense to be included in this class' responsibilities. There may be undiscovered class(es) or misplaced responsibilities. Look carefully at method names and ask yourself questions such as,

Is this something I would expect this class to do?

Is there a less obvious class, such as an event, that has not been defined?

Focus on public methods of a class.

■ Other metrics

Take a look at the *instance variable usage* metric to see if there is a way to divide the class along optimum method lines.

Number of instance variables in a class

The number of instance variables in a class is one measure of its size. Instance variables include *private* and *protected* variables[10] available to the instances.

Meaning

The fact that a class has more instance variables indicates that the class has more relationships to other objects in the system. These may be simple objects, such as strings and integers, or complex domain objects, such as accounts and inventories.

Project results

The results are contained in the section on *average number of instance variables per class.*

Affecting factors

■ Real-world object attributes

Think about the real-world object that this class models. Does it have a large number of attributes? If so, this will al-

---

[10]I do not believe in *public* instance variables, since that breaks encapsulation. If you use them, include them in this count.

leviate some design quality concerns about larger numbers of instance variables.

■ Computed or delegated values

Think about whether an attribute value can be computed when requested (and still meet requirements such as performance). Think about whether this object should hold this value or whether another object should be asked for the value.

■ Passive "data" objects

Some objects take a passive role in the system, existing largely to provide information to other objects as needed. These "data" objects will often have more instance variables to hold their attributes. The instance variables are often base objects, such as strings and integers. An example of a passive object is a *Customer,* which can be asked for her *name, address, ssn,* and other information.

■ Key classes

Key classes tend to be central points of coordination across a number of objects. This coordination often surfaces as instance variables that hold another (key) object.

■ UI classes

Classes that deal with interfaces usually have more instance variables, since they deal with the model object(s) being manipulated, any current selections, as well as any remembered data values entered by the user.

Related metrics

■ Number of methods per class

Thresholds

■ Nine for UI classes

UI classes need more instance variables in order to deal with the screen components, such as listboxes.

■ Three for model classes

There is evidence that classes are more reusable when they have fewer instance variables. Also, I am a big believer in driving my designs by the services that classes are responsible for, rather than the data that they maintain. I firmly believe that systems derived with this focus are easier to develop and maintain. So, I think it is a good rule of thumb for this reason, as well as distribution of intelligence among several self-managing objects, to keep the number of instance variables lower.

Suggested actions

Look for unnecessary object relationships. Look for new, undiscovered classes in your business domain. See if some of the values being kept in instance variables should be computed or can be requested from another object.

Average number of instance variables per class

Across the project, one indication of class size is the average number of instance variables. This will affect the storage requirements for the runtime system as well as any persistent data store, such as an ODBMS.

Meaning

More instance variables, on average, indicate a possibility that the classes are doing more than they should. Due to this fact, the classes may have too many relationships to other objects in the system.

Project results

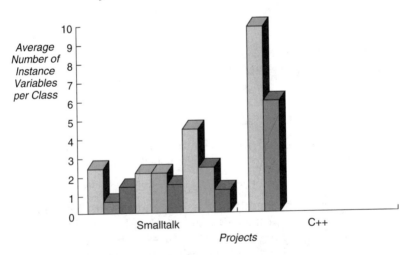

$$\frac{\text{total number of instance variables}}{\text{total number of methods}}$$

Affecting factors

None known at this time. Even though the data points in the preceding chart show higher numbers for C++, I believe this metric should be language independent.

Related metrics

Average number of methods per class.

Thresholds

My threshold for model classes is 3 and for UI classes is 9. UI classes are generally going to need more variables to hold the objects they are working with in the view. There is evidence that smaller numbers of instance variables lead to higher levels of reuse.

Suggested actions

Look for unnecessary object relationships. Look for undiscovered classes. See if some objects held in instance variables should be requested from other objects.

Number of class methods in a class

Classes themselves are objects that can provide services (and state data) that are global to their instances. This makes sense to handle common constant values and instance initialization but should not be the primary way that the work gets done.

Meaning

The number of methods available to the class and not its instances affects the size of the class. The number should generally be relatively small compared to the number of instance methods.

The number of class methods can indicate the amount of commonalty being handled for all instances. It can also indicate poor design if services better handled by individual instances are handled by the class itself. An indication that this is occurring is an abundance of conditional logic based on data values.

Project results

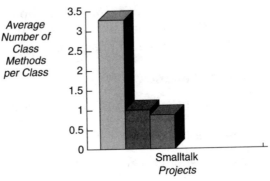

Average Number of Class Methods per Class

Smalltalk Projects

total number of class methods
total number of classes

Affecting factors

■ Class variables

The amount of information that is global to the class' instance objects will affect the number of class methods.

■ Language

C++ classes will normally have extra class methods to handle instance construction and destruction, such as to initialize memory (these are not normally needed in Smalltalk). This metric needs to allow an offset of anomaly threshold values when C++ is being used.

■ Project conventions

You may have conventions, such as the definition of a *class-Comment* or *example* class method, where you would want to utilize offset values.

Related metrics

■ Number of instance methods

■ Number of class variables

Thresholds

I use two types of thresholds:

■ Absolute

Based on project experiences, I use a threshold of four class methods to decide when to look closer at this metric. Classes rarely need more than four class methods.

■ Relative to *number of instance methods*

This works better as a threshold when the class has a more extensive set of methods. It works less well when a class is a minor specialization of a superclass, since a single class method can overwhelm the number of instance methods on a percentage basis.

I use a threshold of 20 percent to identify possible anomalies. This comes from the thresholds for this metric and the threshold for the *number of instance methods* metric (4 versus 20 methods, or 20 percent).

Suggested actions

■ Review the class methods, looking for behavior that should be specific to instances of the class. In general, the vast majority of behavior should be performed by instance objects. Class behavior exists to help in instance creation and to provide behavior that is global to all instances, regardless of the state of the instance data. Instances share the instance behavior too, but they are affected by their specific state data values.

■ Examples of valid uses of class methods:

• Common customization values

There are cases where you will want to tailor the behavior of all instances of a class based on some value setting.

• Display behavior

Attributes such as a type string for a class of objects to show after the name on the display.

Number of class variables in a class

Meaning

Class variables are localized globals, providing common objects to all the instances of a class. There are usually a relatively low number of class variables compared to instance variables. The class variables are often used to provide customizable constant values that are used to affect all the instances' behavior. They might coordinate information across all instances, such as the determination of a unique value for a transaction number.

Project results

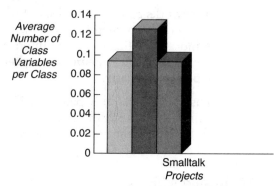

$$\frac{\text{total number of class variables}}{\text{total number of classes}}$$

The average number of class variables should be low. Some classes may have larger numbers of class variables, but in general there should be fewer class variables than instance variables.

Affecting factors

■ The number of customizable features

Systems with a lot of built-in customization will tend to have more class variables to allow the system's behavior to be affected during production.

Related metrics

■ Number of instance variables

■ Number of class methods

Thresholds

On an individual class basis, I use 3 as a threshold to identify anomalies that warrant further examination. For an average threshold, the number should be much lower. As the measured projects show, the *average* number of class variables should be less than 0.1.

Suggested actions

■ Make sure that the focus of the work is done by instances and not the classes themselves. Make sure that the objects kept in class variables contain information common to all instances of that class. Redesign the class if necessary, moving responsibilities to the instances themselves, calculating values when needed, or asking another object for a value.

Class Inheritance

This group of metrics looks at the quality of the classes' use of inheritance.

Class hierarchy nesting level

Classes are organized for inheritance purposes hierarchically in a tree structure, with the base or topmost class called the root.[11] The further down from the root that a class exists in this hierarchy is called its nesting level.

Meaning

Deep class inheritance nesting is not necessary or desirable. Testing is more difficult and the real world does not typically contain this much specialization.

The deeper a class is nested in the inheritance hierarchy, the more public and protected methods there are for the class and the more chances for method overrides or extensions. This all results in greater difficulty in testing a class.

Large nesting numbers indicate a design problem, where developers are overly zealous in finding and creating objects. This will usually result in subclasses that are not specializations of all the superclasses. A subclass should ideally extend the functionality of the superclasses.

Project results

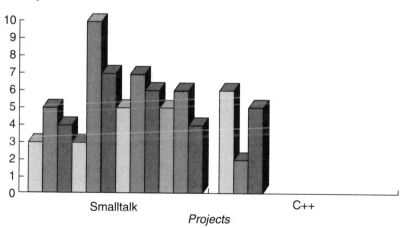

These maximum levels of nesting include the use of frameworks.

---

[11]C++ allows for multiple inheritance, which is not recommended. See the appropriate section in this book for a discussion of multiple inheritance.

Affecting factors

■ Frameworks

Frameworks are groups of classes that work together to provide a partially complete solution to some set of functionality. The most common example of a general-purpose framework is an application UI framework. For example, the *Smalltalk/V*™ system comes with a *ViewManager* class. You create windows by subclassing this class. In addition, projects will often set up their own UI framework underneath. So, the hierarchy you are given to create a view class might look like this:

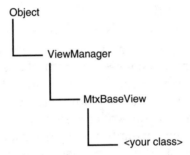

This means that you are starting at a nesting level of 3. This will certainly affect the maximum level you will reach.

There are other frameworks you will find in your model. For example, at Hatteras, we have many frameworks set up for the abstractions found in the problem domain.

I have found that whatever level you start from, you will have at most 6 levels of nesting for your classes. Few levels mean you are not finding the abstractions and specializations to optimize reuse through inheritance. More levels mean you are possibly not subclassing by specialization (is-a).

Related metrics

■ Number of methods in a class

Thresholds

■ Six (from the top of the class hierarchy or the bottom of the framework)

Suggested actions

■ Make sure subclassing is by type.

In the real world that we are modeling, we do not have large numbers of specializations. Think about transportation—we have

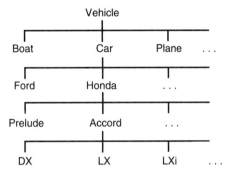

but we don't have useful specializations after this.

Your application will be the same. Looking across a large number of projects and classes, including the Smalltalk system itself, we have seen that there is a natural limit to the ideal class hierarchy nesting level.[12]

■ Look at inherited state and behavior usage.

Subclasses that are divided along lines of what methods and instance variables they use are possible groupings for separate class hierarchy mini-trees.

If the classes involved go across subsystems and/or teams, design reviews will be necessary to communicate the changes.

■ Factor out base classes.

Look for application classes that should be base classes (e.g., String or Integer).

■ See if subclasses should be peer classes.

If a subclass is logically at the same level as a superclass, make them peers under the same superclass. For example, it makes sense for *CDAccount* to be a subclass of *SavingsAccount,* but *SavingsAccount* and *CheckingAccount* should be peers under *Account.*

---

[12]For a further look at this topic, see Mark Lorenz, "Real World Reuse," *Journal of Object-Oriented Programming* (Nov./Dec. 1991).

■ See if subclass and superclass should be merged.

Sometimes, in rapid prototyping, we create a subclass to try something out without changing the existing system. If this subclass should be merged into the superclass, make sure to go back and clean it up.

Number of abstract classes

An abstract class exists to facilitate reuse of methods and state data among its subclasses. It has no instances in a running system but represents a generalization of the concepts embodied in the collection of subclasses.

Meaning

While a superclass does not have to be abstract, experience shows that some number of abstract classes exist in successful projects. The number of abstract classes is an indication of the successful usage of inheritance and the effort that has been spent looking for general concepts in the problem domain.

Project results

Well-designed projects I examine by hand typically have over 10 percent abstract classes.

Affecting factors

■ Frameworks

Frameworks, by definition, typically have a number of abstract classes. This may reduce the number of abstract classes you create in your application.

Related metrics

■ Class hierarchy nesting level

Thresholds

Ten to fifteen percent of your classes should be abstract.

Suggested actions

Group classes of similar type. If you have a group of classes that support different communication protocols, they can possibly be grouped under a *Communication* superclass.

Look for common methods in classes. Pull commonality out to a higher level in the hierarchy, creating a new class with a less-specific name. For example, *CheckingAccount* and *SavingsAccount* could have an *Account* superclass, with methods such as *deposit:* and *withdraw:*.

Use of multiple inheritance

Some languages, such as C++, allow for a class to inherit state and behavior from multiple superclasses. Some would argue that this is necessary to model the real world accurately. Other languages, such as Smalltalk, support only single inheritance (from one superclass).

There are complications that result from using multiple inheritance:

- Name collisions

  If two direct superclasses both have a *balance* method, which method should *anAccount* execute?

- Developer understanding

  When trying to understand a class, working up through two or more inheritance trees is more difficult. Also, trying to maintain the system, including new class placement, becomes more difficult.

The industry has generally agreed that multiple inheritance is not necessary, since there are a number of appropriate ways to model your business, and multiple inheritance introduces possible problems. I recommend that you don't use multiple inheritance. If you do use it, make it a conscious decision and not a general guideline. I include this as a metric because I want to detect its use, since I consider it an anomaly.

Meaning

Classes that inherit from multiple superclasses introduce the possibility of problems. Use of multiple inheritance in languages that support it can be measured and reported to ensure a conscious decision to use it.

Project results

I don't have numbers to offer you, since there have been very few C++ projects I have been involved with that have used multiple inheritance. I advise the projects I work with to avoid using multiple inheritance, since I believe the net result to the project is negative. This is due to the tradeoff of a more difficult design for developers to understand and technical implications, such as name collisions, all for a technique that is not required to model any situation I have come across. Don't get me wrong—there have been a couple of times I could have used multiple inheritance to come up with a (seemingly) more elegant design. Looking back, though, I'm fine with the self-imposed limitation of single inheritance. For example, I've used techniques such as a *Person* having multiple *Roles,* like manager and salesperson, to handle these situations.

Affecting factors

■ Product requirements

Some products rely on multiple inheritance to implement services such as object persistence. If you must use it for this reason, limit your usage to the requirements of the product.

Related metrics

■ Class inheritance nesting level

Thresholds

I use a threshold of zero for the use of multiple inheritance. I put it in the list of metrics because I don't believe in its use and therefore want to detect its usage.

Suggested actions

■ Avoid using multiple inheritance in your designs. Make it a project standard that any uses of multiple inheritance that are deemed necessary must be justified.

Method Inheritance

This group of metrics examines superclass-subclass inheritance relationships.

Number of methods overridden by a subclass

A subclass is allowed to define a method of the same name as a method in one of its superclasses. This is called overriding the method, since a message will now cause the new method to execute instead of the superclass' method.

Meaning

Subclasses should be a specialization of their superclasses.

A large number of overridden methods indicates a design problem. Since a subclass should be a specialization of its superclasses, it should primarily extend the services of the superclasses. This should result in unique new method names. Numerous overrides indicate subclassing for the convenience of reusing some code and/or instance variables when the new subclass is not purely a specialized type of its superclasses.

Project results

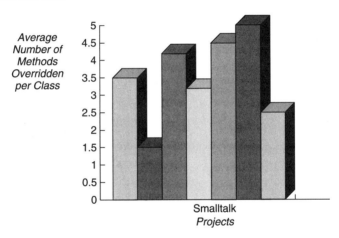

total number of overridden methods
----
total number of classes

The two highest averages in the graph above use multiple frameworks in their projects.

Affecting factors

Some methods are meant to be overridden in planned cases of reuse.

■ Frameworks

Frameworks, as used in this context, are sets of classes that provide some basic functionality that is meant to be the basis for specific reuse in a new application. Often, the framework will define methods that are empty or meant to be overridden in new subclasses. This is certainly not a design flaw. On the contrary, it is a source of great power in developing an application, since it fosters reuse as the original designer intended.

For example, we use our own base UI class to define methods that are meant to be overridden by subclasses:

- *title*   Return aString to use in the view title line.
- *appInitialize*   Perform any view-specific setup.
- *updateMenus*   Enable/disable menus based on the current view selections.
- *currentObject* and *currentObject:*   Get and set the object the view was opened on (single document interface or SDI).

The base class also provides a number of methods for all its subclasses without their overriding any base class stubs.

■ Abstract classes

Similar to frameworks, abstract classes often define methods that are meant to be overridden by their subclasses. In fact, systems such as Smalltalk allow this contract to be enforced by a special message in the superclass method.[13]

If possible, these methods that are intended to be overridden should not be counted toward this metric.

■ Invocation of superclass method

If the superclass' method is invoked, the subclass is essentially extending and not overriding the service. In this case, these method "overrides" should not be counted.

Related metrics

- ■ Class inheritance nesting level
- ■ Number of methods inherited

Thresholds

The number of methods overridden by a subclass *that are not meant to be overridden* (e.g., are not framework placeholder methods) should be three or less. This number should be even smaller for classes nested deeper in the inheritance hierarchy. Larger numbers indicate subclassing by convenience to reuse some methods and/or state data without a strong *is-a* relationship.

---

[13]See the *subclassResponsibility* message, for example.

Suggested actions

Look at the positioning of classes that use a lot of unintended method overrides. They are probably not specializations of the superclasses. Place them under the root *Object* class, under some framework if applicable, or under some class that they specialize.

Number of methods inherited by a subclass

Inheritance is an important concept in developing OO software. Subclasses naturally inherit behavior in the form of methods, and state data in the form of instance variables from their superclasses. This is the normal scheme of the class hierarchy.

Meaning

The number of methods inherited from superclass(es) indicates the strength of the subclassing by specialization.

Project results

No substantial numbers have been collected yet for this metric. In general, the vast majority of methods should be inherited from the superclasses.

Affecting factors

- Method extension

    Methods can override superclass methods to extend the services provided, while still invoking the superclass method.

```
interest
    "Extend basic savings interest with penalties for early CD withdrawal"

interest := super interest.
self subtractAnyPenaltiesFrom: interest.
^interest
```

Related metrics

- Number of methods overridden
- Number of methods added

Thresholds

The percentage of methods inherited should be high. This is the inverse of the *number of methods overridden* threshold. A low percentage of inherited methods indicates poor subclassing.

Suggested actions

If most methods are not inherited, look at the type of object a class represents. See if it can fit better under another class or if it should be subclassed directly under a framework class or a root class such as *Object*.

Number of methods added by a subclass

This is the normal expectation for a subclass—that it will further specialize the superclass' type of object.

Meaning

Subclasses should define new methods, extending the behavior of the superclass(es). A class with no methods is certainly questionable (although organizing classes for the developers may be justification enough in some cases).

The number of new methods should usually decrease as you move down through the layers of the hierarchy.

Project results

Numbers for this metric have not been systematically collected, largely because other metrics have overshadowed it. The anomalies detected with this metric are usually detected by the *number of methods overridden* metric, for example.

Affecting factors

■ Depth in the inheritance hierarchy

   The farther down in the inheritance hierarchy, the more a new subclass has available for its use. This results in less need for new methods (in general).

Related metrics

■ Number of methods overridden

■ Class hierarchy nesting level

Thresholds

The lower threshold is one, since all classes should have at least one method to justify their existence.

The upper threshold is actually a declining scale, based on the *class hierarchy nesting level*. Since I don't have detailed numbers from measured projects, I hesitate to quote a scale here. One data point we have is the *number of instance methods in a class* metric threshold of 20. So, at a nesting level of 1, the number of new methods threshold should be 20. We also know, from the *class hierarchy nesting level* metric, that the maximum nesting level should be around six. So, at a nesting level of six, the number of new methods threshold should be low, say below four.

Suggested actions

For deeply nested subclasses with large numbers of methods, see if some of them can be moved higher in the class hierarchy, allowing more classes to reuse the logic. Ask yourself:

Does the service provided by the method make sense at a higher level?

Can the method be redesigned to allow for custom adaptations to a basic behavior?

Specialization index

Pure specialization implies adding more behavior while completely utilizing the existing behavior as is. In practice, specialization through subclassing includes

- adding new methods.
- adding behavior to existing methods, while still invoking the superclass method.
- overriding methods with totally new behavior.
- deleting methods by overriding them with no behavior.

Meaning

By looking at a combination of metrics, we can make a determination of the quality of the subclassing. In this case, *quality* is defined as

high = subclassing by specialization
low   = implementation subclassing

Subclassing by specialization means an extension of the capabilities of the superclasses, creating a new type of object that *is-a* superset of the superclasses. This desirable type of subclassing is characterized by

■ low numbers of method overrides.

■ decreasing numbers of added methods.

■ few or no deleted methods.

Implementation subclassing is a convenient usage of some portion of the behavior and/or state data in the superclasses by a subclass that is not the same type of object as the superclasses. This undesirable type of subclassing results in brittle relationships that break as changes are made.

Project results

I have measured a number of projects using this index calculation for each class:

$$\frac{\text{number of overridden methods} * \text{class hierarchy nesting level}}{\text{total number of methods}}$$

This weighted calculation has done a good job of identifying classes worth looking at for their placement in the inheritance hierarchy and for design problems.

Affecting factors

■ Class hierarchy nesting level

The farther down in the class hierarchy you go, the more specialized the (sub)class should be. Therefore, overridden methods bear more weight toward reaching an anomaly threshold than for a class higher in the inheritance hierarchy.

■ Frameworks

Some methods are meant to be overridden and should not be included in this count.

Related metrics

■ Number of methods overridden by a subclass

■ Number of methods inherited by a subclass

■ Number of methods added by a subclass

Thresholds

I use 15 percent as an anomaly threshold, which results in a maximum of three overridden methods at the first level of nesting (*number of overridden methods* threshold) and less overrides at higher nesting levels.

Suggested actions

Verify the class location in the inheritance hierarchy. Ask yourself:

> *Is this class the same kind of thing as its superclass(es)?*
>
> *Do the override methods invoke the superclass' method?*

No to the above questions means the class should probably be moved elsewhere in the hierarchy.

Class Internals ─────────────────────

This set of metrics looks at the design of the classes' internals—how they use their instance variables, what external references they make, and so on.

Class cohesion

The message connections within a class and the use of instance variables are certainly forms of cohesion. Since cohesion is desirable, a candidate metric is to measure the amount of cohesion within a class as a design metric.

Meaning

Cohesion in anthropomorphic OO system views has to do with the logical allocation of behavior to objects within that system. Unfortunately, that viewpoint takes human intervention. In order to find automatable measurements, other metrics are needed for cohesion.

The interrelationships among the class' methods and the patterns of variable usage by methods relate to the cohesion of the class.

Project results

[CHID91] looked at class cohesion. Specifically, patterns of instance variable usage by methods are an input into the determination of the cohesion across a class. This defines possible boundaries to divide a class with poor cohesion into multiple classes.

Affecting factors

None known at this time.

Related metrics

- Class coupling

Thresholds

None at this time.

Suggested actions

Variable references by methods is one input to consider if you are trying to decide how to divide up a class that is too large or contains multiple "personalities."

Global usage

Globals come in multiple flavors:

- System globals

  These are global to the entire system. Generally, you may need one system global to "bootstrap" your system at startup. This object will usually be a system object, such as a *Store* object, that models the overall enterprise being automated.

- Class variables

  These are global to the instances of a class. They are typically used to keep data that should be common across all instances, such as a font to use or a symbol name. Class variables are typically much less common than instance variables.

- Pool dictionaries

  These are global to any classes which include them as a "common" area. They are used for standard values such as print control characters.

In general, global usage should be minimized as in traditional development. More use of globals indicates poor object-oriented design. There are some global references that are intentional (beyond the "system" object). For example, to support a build process, you may see code in Smalltalk such as:

```
( Smalltalk at: #HatterasSoftware ) new
```

My friend and OO aficionado Bob Brodd thinks this is a poor technique, corrupting a design to support ease of building the system.[14] But, that is a topic for another book—perhaps next year.

Meaning

Globals make knowledge of objects available to all objects in the system, encouraging unnecessary coupling.

Project results

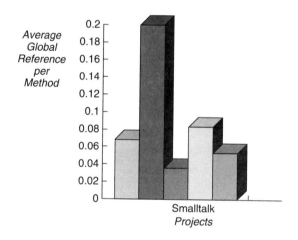

$$\frac{\text{total number of global references}}{\text{total number of methods}}$$

Affecting factors

None.

Related metrics

- Number of class variables

[14]The reason for the indirect reference to the class name is so you don't have to worry about the order of filing in parts of the system during a build. A class reference before the class is defined results in an error.

Thresholds

I use an upper threshold of one system global to identify anomalies.

Suggested actions

Justify any global references other than one "system" global.

Average number of parameters per method

The tradeoff between parameter passing and instance variable usage in some cases has to do with how object relationships are maintained (via pointers). In other cases, it has to do with how much is expected of client code in order to use some functionality.

Meaning

Parameters require more effort of clients.

Project results

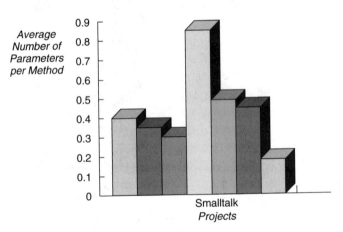

$$\frac{\text{total number of method parameters}}{\text{total number of methods}}$$

Affecting factors

- Setting access methods

  By definition, a setting access method has a parameter.

- Architected protocols

  Predefined protocols that are expected to be supported can be used in lieu of parameters.

Related metrics

None.

Thresholds

An upper threshold of 0.7 parameters per method, based on project results.

Suggested actions

High and low numbers of parameters imply a style of design. Higher numbers put a heavier burden on the client. Watch for gross differences in the use of parameters and examine why the numbers are so different.

Use of friend functions

Some languages, such as C++, allow you to write code that breaks the encapsulation of objects.

Meaning

Friends allow encapsulation to be violated. They are needed in some (very few) cases, such as support for commutative expressions. Other uses should be justified.

Project results

I don't have statistics on the use of friend functions.

Affecting factors

- Mathematical operators

  Operators such as multiplication and addition need to use friend functions in C++ to support the commutative law.

Related metrics

None.

Thresholds

I use zero as an upper threshold for friend functions.

Suggested actions

Justify any use of friend functions that are not for mathematical operators' support of commutative expressions.[15]

---

[15]The commutative law says that **a** * **b** is the same as **b** * **a.** This allows client code to ignore the order of the objects in an expression.

Percentage of function-oriented code

Some languages, such as C++, allow the developer to write code outside of objects. An obvious example is in the C++ *main* routine.

Meaning

Non-OO code in general can be viewed as a design problem, indicating a regression to function-oriented coding.

Project results

None.

Affecting factors

■ Language

Some languages may necessitate or encourage the use of logic outside of objects.

Related metrics

None.

Thresholds

■ While I understand that there is a pragmatic need for procedural code in some languages, I set an upper threshold of zero and require justification for its use so that a conscious decision is made.

Suggested actions

■ Review *main* routines

Main routines should be used to get the application started, and nothing more.

■ Require justification for non-OO code

Any code written outside the class structure should be justified.

Average number of comment lines per method

Meaning

On average, a class' methods should have at least one comment line. While some methods, such as accessing methods, may not need a comment, others will need more than one line. Looking at commented method percentages will indicate whether enough comments are being entered. Comments due to project conventions or tool automatic insertion, such as initials and date, should not be counted as explanatory comments.

Project results

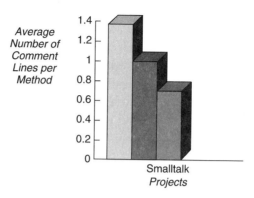

$$\frac{\text{total number of comment lines}}{\text{total number of methods}}$$

These numbers have had the project initials/timestamp lines automatically put into the methods for those projects that followed this convention. They have not had accessing methods factored out of the percentages though, so the level of commentary for those methods that really need explanation is really somewhat higher.

Affecting factors

■ Project conventions and tools

Projects often have conventions, such as the insertion of initials and timestamp, as a comment line in all methods.

■ Accessing methods

Methods that simply return an instance variable don't generally need commentary.

Related metrics

■ Average number of commented methods

Thresholds

I use a lower threshold of one to identify anomalies.

Suggested actions

Require that developers include descriptive commentary in their methods.

Average number of commented methods

This percentage indicates the amount of overall commentary included in the methods. A method counts toward the percentage if it has *any* comments in it.

Meaning

On average, a class' methods should have at least one comment line. While some methods, such as accessing methods, may not need a comment, others will need more than one line. Looking at commented method percentages will indicate whether enough comments are being entered. Comments due to project conventions or tool automatic insertion, such as initials and date, should not be counted as explanatory comments.

Project results

The chart shows the average percentage of methods with comments.

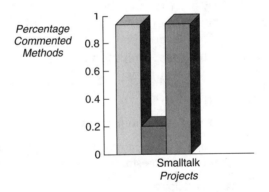

$$\frac{\text{total number of methods with comments}}{\text{total number of methods}}$$

Affecting factors

■ Accessing methods

Accessing methods do not normally need commentary. For example, the code does not need a comment to explain what it is doing. Factoring out accessing methods will provide a more meaningful measure of the amount of commentary in the methods.

■ Automatic date/time stamps

Many environments automatically put initials and a date/time stamp as a comment in a new method. For example, the code

```
averagePrice
        "MEL 6/30/93"

    | totalPrice |
    totalPrice := 0.
    ( products ) do: [ :each |
        totalPrice := totalPrice + each price.
        ].
    ^totalPrice / ( products size )
```

does not contain a descriptive comment, even though there is a comment in the code. Factoring out generic commentary will provide a more meaningful measure of the amount of commentary in the methods.

Related metrics

None.

Thresholds

I use a lower threshold of 65 percent and an upper threshold of 100 percent to identify anomalies for this metric.

Suggested actions

Any classes that have less than 50 percent of their meaningful methods (see *affecting factors* above) commented should have commentary added by the class owner.

Number of problem reports per class or contract

Meaning

Certainly, classes with larger numbers of problem reports against them are candidates for rewrite, due to

■ additional unplanned requirements.

■ poor design.

Project results

My customers, the commercial products' managers, and my company are all guilty of not correlating problem reports to classes and/or contracts. If we had these statistics, we could decide more efficiently what areas of the system need redesign.

Affecting factors

None.

Related metrics

None.

Thresholds

I would suggest a threshold of one for contracts and two for classes. Additional problem reports should trigger a broader look at the situation.

Suggested actions

There's not much you can do as far as new requirements are concerned to prepare yourself. You can keep track of the least-understood areas of the system, which have an above-average probability of being hit by new or better understood requirements.

Areas of the system that were poorly designed the first time need to be reworked with the mentoring of better-skilled developers.

Class Externals

This set of metrics examines how the class relates to other classes, subsystems, users, and so on.

Class coupling

The message connections between classes are certainly forms of coupling. Since coupling in general is not desirable, a candidate metric is to measure the amount of coupling between classes as a design metric.

There are multiple ways to measure the coupling:

- The number of other classes collaborated with, and

- The amount of collaboration with other classes.

It seems at odds that we want to build systems that get their work done by requesting services from other objects and yet keep the amount of coupling to a minimum. It becomes clearer if you think of it this way: You want to leverage the other classes' services, but you want to have services available at the right level, so that you know only about a limited number of objects and their services. They, in turn, request services from other objects you don't know about to get their work done, and so on throughout however many objects are necessary. If you had to interact with all the indirectly related objects, we'd have a tangled web of interdependencies and maintenance would be a nightmare.

Meaning

Coupling between classes relates to the interrelationships that bind the two together. In effect, the coupling is determined by the level of dependencies between the classes.

[BOYD93] defines coupling thus:

*When one object depends implicitly on another, they are **tightly** coupled. Object instances are tightly coupled with their classes. When one object depends directly on the visibility of another, they are **closely** coupled. Smalltalk instance, class, and pool variables are closely coupled to the instances that reference them. When one object references another only indirectly through . . . the other's public interface [they are] **loosely** coupled.*

Project results

None available.

Affecting factors

■ Frameworks

Coupling between classes in the framework is defined by the architected interfaces built into the framework. This is the predefined mechanism for how the benefits of the framework can be garnered.

■ Inheritance

By definition, subclasses are tightly coupled to their superclass(es). There are ways you can minimize this coupling too, such as by the use of *accessing* methods and (in C++) *private* methods. I agree that *accessing* methods are desirable, since they insulate the subclasses from changes to the implementation details. I do not agree that subclasses that are true specializations of the superclass(es) should not have access to methods of the superclass(es). In other words, I have not been convinced that C++ *private* methods should be used. I would stick to *protected* methods.

■ Use of globals

Globals are brittle dependencies that will cause you maintenance headaches. You will probably need one "system" global to bootstrap your application. Any globals beyond that should be justified.

Related metrics

None.

Thresholds

None at this time.

Suggested actions

Reuse encourages lower levels of coupling. Inheritance encourages higher levels of coupling. Look at the most important purposes for a class to determine which path to take.

Number of times a class is reused

Reuse is a complex subject. I was involved in setting up the reuse plan for an 850-person IBM lab, so I realize that most of the problems with getting real improvements in the level of software reuse are not technical issues.

There are a number of ways to count reuse, including white box and black box reuse:

■ White box

Reusing software through the examination of the internals of the component. White box reuse often takes the form of copying and pasting pieces of code from another component. Additional work is required for finishing the development, testing, documentation, and maintenance.

■ Black box

Reusing functionality through a defined interface to it, without examining the internals of the component. The reused off-the-shelf component doesn't need testing, documentation, or separate maintenance.

One of the key benefits of OO is the additional support for reuse. Everything you do in an OO system is accomplished by requesting services from (reusing!) other objects. You actually use both white box and black box reuse to do this.

Meaning

The number of references to a class. The number of applications using a class. Planning for a second use during development of candidate classes has been successful in developing more reusable classes and frameworks the first time.

Project results

None.

Affecting factors

■ Place in the inheritance hierarchy

From an implementation standpoint, classes do not stand on their own. They often rely on a great deal of work that occurred higher in the hierarchy (through inheritance) as well as elsewhere in the hierarchy (through delegation).

Related metrics

None.

Thresholds

Every project should have a set of classes that are to be submitted to the company's reuse library. Every project should have a set of classes that are to be reused from the reuse library, rather than built from scratch (once a reuse library is populated, of course!).

Suggested actions

■ Focus reuse investment in key classes that are explicitly selected for submission to the reuse library. This implies

- more testing.
- more documentation.
- less coupling.

■ Plan for a second use of a set of classes during the initial development. This has proven effective at producing a more reusable set of classes the first time out.

Number of classes/methods thrown away

I catch a lot of heat on a regular basis for talking about throwing something away. I have refused to soften the wording because I firmly believe that true iterations on designs are absolutely critical to the development of really elegant solutions. Experience is the best way to understand a domain.

I am not proposing that everything be thrown out. In fact, the most important assets in any work will never be thrown away—the key classes, their responsibilities, relationships to other classes, and increased understanding of the domain. I am only focusing on the importance of recognizing the different focuses during analysis and design iterations.

I believe that measuring this metric has value and that if nothing is being thrown away and something else is being designed, the project is stagnating. I have seen on multiple occasions the increased quality of reworking areas of systems. The all-time champion at this technique is my friend Bob Brodd. He is great at reworking systems to get jumps in quality and resilience . . . and the iterations go faster and faster with more and more functionality delivered.

Meaning

Developers don't get designs right the first time. Part of iterating is learning about the domain and design and building it better the next time.

Project results

[WEST92] reports reductions in the number of classes and methods per class over time on multiple C++ projects. Every OO project I have been involved with has seen similar events during the course of the project.

Affecting factors

None known.

Related metrics

None.

Thresholds

In any project I was managing, I would look for some number of classes and methods being deleted. If I didn't see any, I would wonder if my team was really iterating or just incrementally adding functionality.

Suggested actions

None at this time.

Recommendations

 We have gone over a lot of candidate metrics that you can use on your project. So, which metrics should you use? As you hopefully know by now, there is not one right answer but merely a set of metrics that have been successfully used in the past. In this section, I give you my recommendations that I would expect you to adapt to your situation.

Local Calibration

Every organization needs to calibrate the metrics across a number of projects. As [KITCH90] says, "Most predictive equations appear to be environment-dependent, and therefore need to be derived from, and validated on, locally collected data." [DEMAR82] suggests that the best way to judge a metric value is by comparison to similar projects, which he describes as "projects produced by the same company, in the same language, which have the same processing bias . . . "

Setting Up a Metrics Program

To use metrics effectively at your company requires you to compile an accurate statistical database across a number of projects.

[BAKER91] lists four steps based on his experiences in setting up a metrics program at your company:

- Define the metrics to collect

   This is the most important step, since it affects the other steps. Select measures that fit your organization's needs. Get management support.

- Convince your organization to collect these metrics

   Choose metrics that are as unobtrusive as possible.

- Automate the metric collection with tools

- Publicize success stories and encourage exchange of ideas

Whatever steps you follow, the most important thing is to measure your software projects, so you can understand what is happening on this project and help future projects at your company develop better estimates and designs.

Metric Recommendations

The following tables indicate my personal recommendations of which metrics from this book to use for which purposes and during which development phases.

Project metrics

The following table maps the project metrics to their potential and recommended uses.

	Estimating	Scheduling	Staffing
Application Size			
Number of scenario scripts (NSS)	✔		
Number of key classes (NKC)	⊠		
Number of support classes (NSC)	✔	✔	✔
Number of subsystems (NOS)	✔	✔	
Staffing Size			
Person-days per class (PDC)	✔		⊠
Classes per developer (CPD)	✔		⊠
Scheduling			
Number of major iterations (NMI)		✔	
Number of contracts completed (NCC)	⊠		

Where:　✔　= the metric applies to this use
　　　　⊠　= the metric is highly recommended for this use

The *number of key classes* can be used to predict the total number of classes in the system. Using *person-days per class* and *classes per developer,* you can then create initial schedule and staffing plans. Progress can be measured by *number of contracts completed.*

The following diagram indicates the development phases to which the recommended project metrics apply:

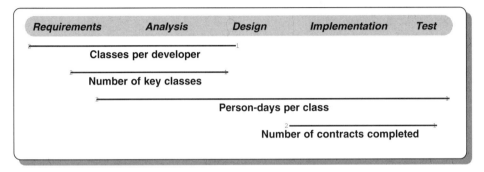

The *classes per developer* metric can be used during early project estimations to help with staffing and scheduling.

The *number of key classes* metric is good for helping to get an early estimate of the total number of classes and effort for the project.

The *person-days per class* metric can be used in conjunction with other measurements, such as the total number of classes, to help with staffing and status for most of the project.

The *number of contracts completed* metric can be used to estimate progress during the latter stages of the detailed design and implementation.

Design metrics

The table on the following pages maps the project metrics to their potential and recommended uses.

Model quality anomalies can be detected by

■ Class hierarchy nesting level

An inheritance hierarchy that is too shallow or too deep has quality repercussions.

■ Global usage

Too many references to globals imply a poor model design.

	Model Quality	Class Quality	Method Quality	Management
Method Size				
Number of message sends (NOM)			⊠	
LInes of code (LOC)			✔	
Method Internals				
Method complexity (MCX)			⊠	
Strings of message sends (SMS)			✔	
Class Size				
Number of public instance methods (PIM)		⊠		⊠
Number of instance methods (NIM)		⊠		
Number of instance variables (NIV)		⊠		
Number of class methods (NCM)		⊠		
Number of class variables (NCV)		✔		
Class Inheritance				
Hierarchy nesting level (HNL)	⊠			
Multiple inheritance (MUI)	⊠			
Method Inheritance				
Number of methods overridden (NMO)		⊠		
Number of methods inherited (NMI)		✔		
Number of methods added (NMA)		✔		
Specialization index (SIX)		⊠		
Class Internals				
Class cohesion (CCO)		✔		
Global usage (GUS)	⊠			
Instance variable usage (IVU)		✔		

	Model Quality	Class Quality	Method Quality	Management
Method Size				
Parameters per method (PPM)		✔		
Friend functions (FFU)	⊠	✔		
Function-oriented code (FOC)	⊠		✔	
Comment lines per method (CLM)		✔		
Percentage of commented methods (PCM)	⊠	⊠		
Problem reports per class (PRC)		⊠		⊠
Class Externals				
Class coupling (CCP)		✔		
Class reuse (CRE)		⊠		⊠
Number of classes thrown away (NCT)				✔
Number of collaborations (NCO)		✔		
Subsystem Coupling				
Intersubsystem relationships (ISR)	⊠			
Interclass relationships (ICR)	✔			

Where: ✔ = the metric applies to this use
        ⊠ = the metric is highly recommended for this use

■ Percentage of commented methods

Little commentary affects the maintainability of the model.

■ Intersubsystem relationships

Large numbers of intersubsystem messages imply a poor choice of subsystem boundaries.

Class quality anomalies can be detected by

■ Number of instance methods

No instance methods or too many instance methods can indicate nonoptimal allocation of responsibility.

■ Number of instance variables

Larger numbers of instance variables can indicate too much coupling with other classes and reduce reuse.

■ Number of class methods

Too many class methods indicate inappropriate use of classes to do work instead of instances.

■ Number of methods overridden

Overriding methods, especially deeper in the hierarchy, can indicate poor subclassing.

■ Specialization index

The specialization index proposed in this book summarizes the inheritance indicators to quantify the subclassing quality.

■ Percentage of commented methods

The method commentary partially indicates how easy maintenance of this class will be.

■ Problem reports per class

Classes with more problem reports are candidates for redesign.

■ Class reuse

Classes that are reused within and across projects are valuable resources to submit to a reuse library. Reuse is one indicator of value.

Method quality anomalies can be detected by

■ Number of message sends

Methods should be short. Longer methods may indicate function-oriented logic.

■ Method complexity

In general, methods should be short and have relatively few conditional blocks.

Management can be helped by

■ Number of public instance methods

Public interface development indicates a level of completion.

■ Class reuse

Reuse won't happen without management support. The greatest software asset a company has is its reuse library of components.

■ Problem reports per class

Classes with higher-than-average numbers of problem reports for this project or the project database are candidates for redesign.

The following diagram indicates the development phases to which the recommended design metrics apply:

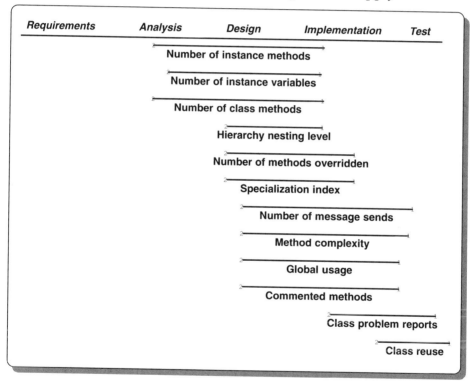

The metrics in this group are meant to help primarily with the later stages of development to ensure a high-quality design and implementation.

Coverage

This book has given you a set of results and recommendations that I have found useful in the OO projects I have been involved in. These are not the final answer but rather a snapshot of OO metrics knowledge at this point in time.

[BAKER91] states that metrics should cover the following:

■ Size

We have certainly discussed a lot of metrics that measure size, such as *number of instance methods* and *number of message sends*.

■ Time

Time is a factor that can be applied to most of the metrics we have discussed, but we didn't directly discuss it for most of the metrics. Time was included in some metrics, such as *person-days per class*. Others can have a time dimension added, such as *problem reports per class* plotted over time.

■ People

People resources are included in metrics such as *classes per developer*.

■ Cost

Cost was not discussed at length in this book. Each company can apply its own overhead costs and developer costs to the metrics.

■ Defects

Problem reports per class is the primary defect metric in the book. It can be extended by looking at time to resolve problems.

So, this book deals to some degree with all these areas except cost. The metrics that are included can help with cost estimates on a company-by-company basis.

Appendixes

Project Experience Database

A sampling of the projects analyzed over the last few years are included here for more detailed inspection. Unfortunately, it is difficult to get approval and cooperation in analyzing a project and publishing the results. The following charts compare the sizes of the projects included in this section. The comparison is based on two metrics:

■ Total number of classes

Over a relatively large project, this metric is fairly accurate for comparing size.

■ Total number of message sends

This is a more indicative measure of the size of the effort.

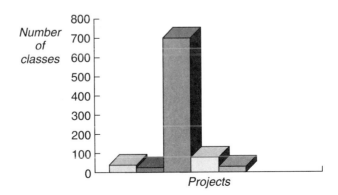

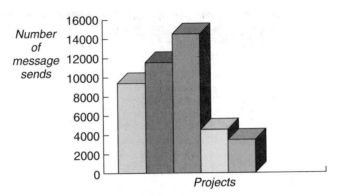

Project 1—WindowBuilder Pro™

*Window-
Builder Pro
has 64
classes and
972 meth-
ods. As with
most
Smalltalk ap-
plications,
much is
done with
relatively few
classes. In
this case, the
original Win-
dowBuilder
classes pro-
vided a head
start, as well
as the
Smalltalk
base
classes.*

Type of application

WindowBuilder Pro™ is a graphical user interface (GUI) development tool for use with Smalltalk/V™ Windows and Smalltalk/V™ OS2. It is generally considered a successful product on the marketplace.

Extent of user interface portion

WindowBuilder Pro™ has a GUI that includes a toolbar, multiple windows, and direct actions via mouse and keyboard.

Length of development effort

ObjectShare president Robert Yerex estimated that 7.5 person-months were spent on WindowBuilder Pro™. He estimated that approximately 4.5 person-months were spent to create the original WindowBuilder™ product. This means that approximately 2.5 person-days were spent on each class. I would assume that part of the reason these numbers are so low is that they were working from a base set of classes.

Effort by phase(s)

Analysis and design	30%
Coding and testing	50%
Documentation, requirements, and so on	20%

Status

WindowBuilder Pro™ has been initially released on Windows™ and OS/2™. WindowBuilder™ was previously released with less function on Windows™ and OS/2™ with two releases on each platform.

Problem reports

The first year's release has seen around 12 problem reports attributable to WindowBuilder Pro™ classes, or about one problem for every 5.4 classes.

Development process

ObjectShare used an *iterative* development process in producing WindowBuilder Pro™, with incrementally added new functions and reworked iterations on existing functions.

The four product developers were responsible for their own unit testing. The function and system testing were performed by 1.5 testers. In addition, a large number of people used the beta prerelease version of the product. Two people were responsible for on-line help and manuals.

Tools used

Smalltalk/V™ was at the core of the product development, as you would expect, since WindowBuilder Pro™ is a Smalltalk development environment tool.

Envy Developer™ is used at ObjectShare, but they used an in-house version control tool for WindowBuilder Pro™ production in order to follow the Smalltalk releases more closely.

Target

WindowBuilder Pro™ currently runs on Windows™ and OS/2™. A Macintosh release is due in early 1994. A Unix version will follow a Smalltalk/V release on Unix.

Target language

Smalltalk/V™ was the only language used in producing WindowBuilder Pro™.

Code product packaging

Source code is included for all versions. The OS/2™ version also includes a DLL file option. The product also comes in Team/V™ and Envy Developer™ versions. A runtime file is also shipped for use with production systems to support the WindowBuilder Pro™ classes with no runtime fees.

Source of metrics numbers

OOMetric™ from Hatteras Software was used to collect the metrics for this product.

Metric results

All in all, WindowBuilder Pro™ did splendidly across the board for the set of metrics collected, with one exception: commentary. The ObjectShare people claim that they intentionally left out much commentary, since they ship source code with their product and don't want to make it too easy for people to understand the finer points of their work.

Number of methods overridden

The few classes with larger numbers of method overrides were mostly within frameworks where methods are designed to be overridden. The average number of methods overridden per class is 4.97.

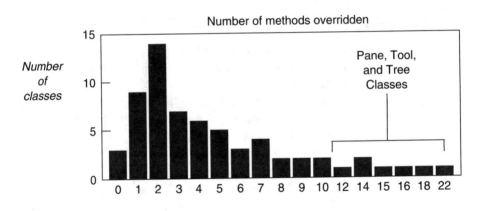

Class hierarchy nesting level

This histogram shows a typical pattern of nesting: enough to gain reuse through abstraction, but not so much as to indicate poor subclassing.

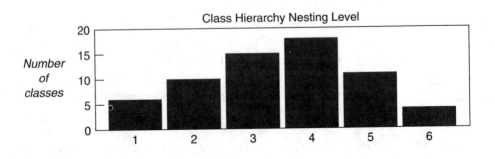

Global usage

References to globals are still generally undesirable. This histogram shows a good pattern to look for in your projects.

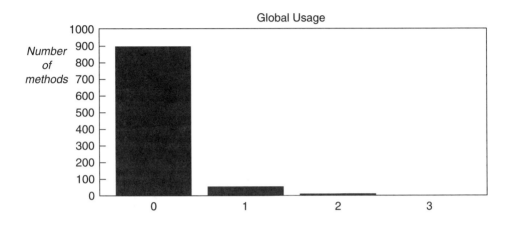

Number of class methods

With a few exceptions, there should be relatively few class methods in your systems, with most of the work being completed by the instance objects.

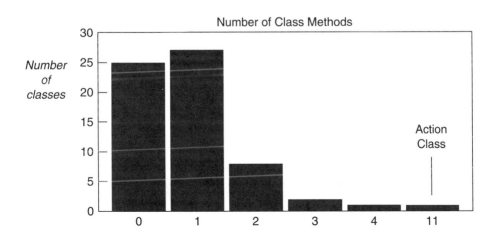

Number of instance variables

UI classes tend to have more state data to handle the complexities of the interfaces on today's systems. In general, the fewer instance variables a class has, the more reusable it is.

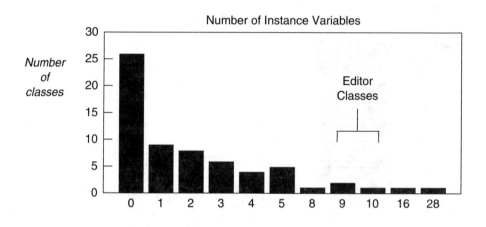

Number of statements

This histogram is a good pattern to look for when measuring your projects. You should see a rapid drop in method size. For Smalltalk, you should try to keep the average size below nine statements.

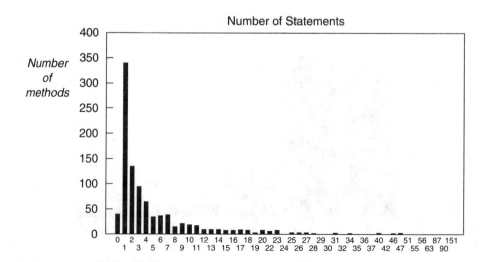

Lines of code

Style issues affect LOC more than other method size metrics. Nevertheless, the pattern should still drop off rapidly.

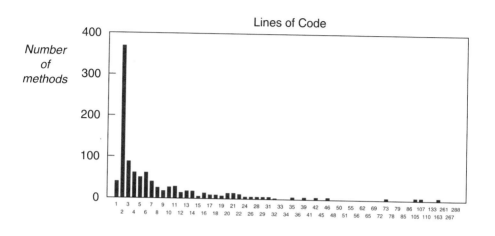

Number of message sends

This method size metric is one of the more accurate ways to measure methods. You should see a less dramatic drop in size compared to other method size metrics. The average number of message sends per method in this histogram is 9.5.

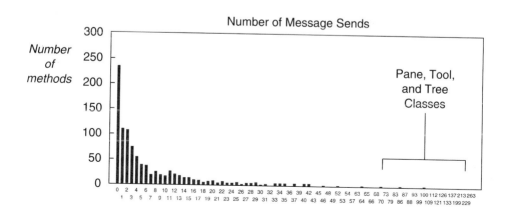

Number of instance methods

We again see the effect of UI classes on a metric. UI classes typically have much larger numbers of instance methods. This is fine for classes with complex interfaces to service. Model classes with high numbers of instance methods (over 20) should be examined carefully. The average number of instance methods per class is 14.4 in this case.

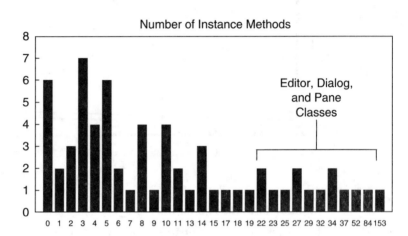

HOMSuite has 36 classes and 1076 methods.

Project 2—HOMSuite™

Type of application

HOMSuite™ is an object-oriented analysis and design CASE tool that supports an extended responsibility driven design (RDD) methodology and scenario scripts. It supports document and Smalltalk and C++ code generation.

Extent of user interface portion

HOMSuite™ has a GUI that includes embedded objects, multiple windows, and direct actions via mouse and keyboard.

Length of development effort

Seven person-months. This means that an average of approximately 4 person-days was needed per production class. The lower number is at least partially attributable to a development staff composed entirely of people with multiple years of experience using OO.

Status

Hatteras Software's HOMSuite™ has been initially released on Windows™.

Development process

Iterative. Multiple iterations with a beta test release were used.

Tools used

Smalltalk/V™ Windows, Microsoft Word™ for on-line help. Release 2: the plan is to also use WindowBuilder Pro™ for the GUI.

Target

Windows™ 3.1+ for release 1; Windows™ 3.1+, OS/2™ 2.1+ for release 2; Unix when a Unix version of Smalltalk/V™ is available.

Target language

Smalltalk/V™ Windows was used for the production code.

Code product packaging

Runtime with no source included, packaged as a combination of EXE and DLL files.

Source of metrics numbers

OOMetric™ from Hatteras Software was used to collect the metrics for this product.

Metric results

Overall, frameworks were effectively used. A number of anomalies were detected, with most of them resolved quickly by looking at affecting factors such as GUI classes. Some metrics bear more investigation, as noted below.

Number of methods overridden

By definition, a framework implies that more methods will be overridden. Within a framework, this is a good indicator. Outside a framework, it indicates inappropriate subclassing. The average number of methods overridden per class is 4.56. This would be high if not for the use of UI, document, and model frameworks.

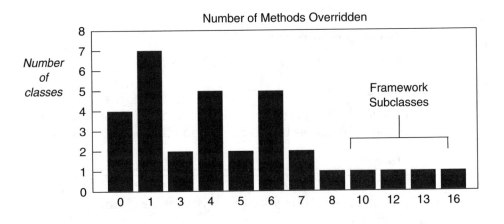

Class hierarchy nesting level

Most hierarchies are under six levels of nesting. Levels below four indicate a need to look for more abstractions; higher levels indicate the possibility of poor subclassing and/or poor class choices.

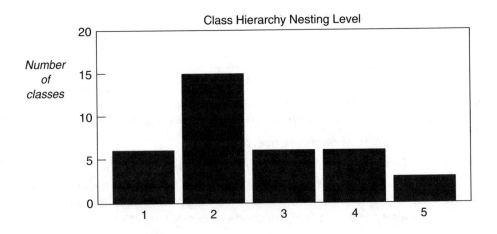

Global usage

Another good pattern—few global references. Most systems have one "system" global and few others. Remember, class and pool variable references are not counted as globals.

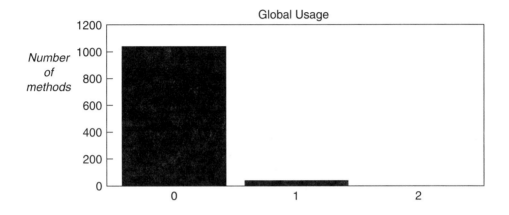

Number of class methods

Class methods should, in general, be far fewer in number than instance methods. This histogram has a class with a large number of class methods. A design decision was made to create a static, "smart" dictionary class to support a generic documentation system tag language. Since the tags do not change, class methods were used. The project also had conventions such as the use of *example* class methods for view classes.

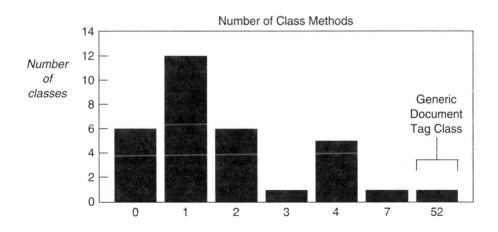

Number of instance variables

Again, the larger numbers are from UI classes. The design could possibly be improved by looking at the model classes in the five-to-eight instance variable range.

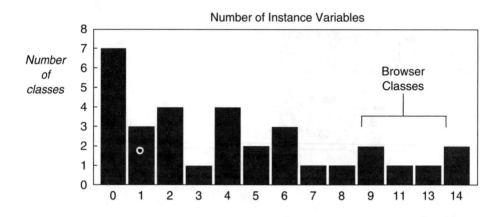

Number of statements

The 10-to-30 statement range methods could possibly be reviewed and improved. The drop in size is not as dramatic as you would like to see.

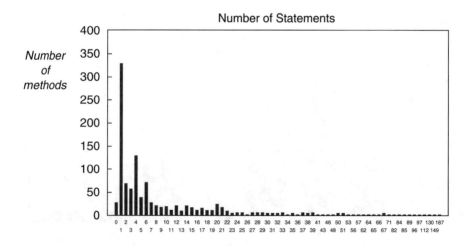

Lines of code

You can see how much style choices affect this metric by comparing it to the *number of message sends* histogram. Be especially careful if you compare your project to other projects using this metric.

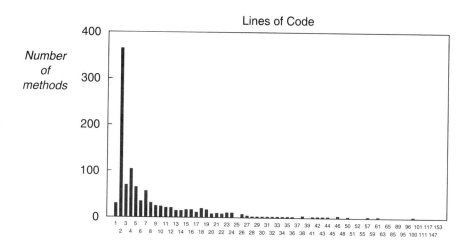

Number of message sends

The average number of message sends per method is 10.77, which is a little high. It is offset by the fact that there are a number of large UI *open* methods which skew the numbers.

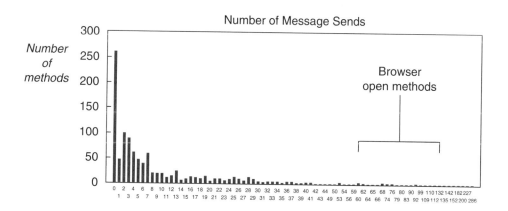

Number of instance methods

The average number of instance methods per class is 22.09, which is a bit high. This is again caused by the UI classes, to manage the GUI interface. This is a case where filtering out the affecting factors removes the anomalies.

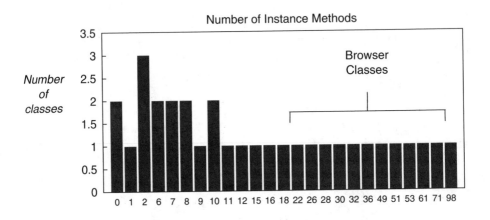

Project 3—Smalltalk/V™ OS2

Type of application

Smalltalk/V™ is an OO development environment that includes browsers, a debugger, and a number of prebuilt classes. It is one of the two dominant versions of Smalltalk on the marketplace, having been sold since 1983. Smalltalk/V Windows alone is reported to have over 10,000 licenses sold.

Extent of user interface portion

Smalltalk/V™ has a GUI that includes multiple windows and direct actions via mouse and keyboard.

Length of development effort

Development team:	5 person-years
Testers:	1+ person-years
Documenters:	1.5 person-years

Most of the effort for this release was in the new 32-bit kernel.

Status

Smalltalk/V™ has been released multiple times on DOS, Windows™, Macintosh™, and OS/2™.

Development process

According to Jeff King, *Digitalk's* director of development, the Smalltalk portion of the product used a "highly iterative" development process. The virtual machine, which is written in C and assembler, used an incremental development process.

Tools used

Kernel:	SDK, compilers, IPMD debugger
Smalltalk:	Smalltalk environment tools

Target

Windows™ and OS/2™.

Target language

Smalltalk.

Secondary language

C and assembly language.

Requirements that necessitated secondary language

Kernel primitives for the environment.

Code product packaging

Most source included. Some kernel methods do not include source.

Source of metrics numbers

OOMetric™ from Hatteras Software was used to collect the metrics for this product.

Metric results

Smalltalk/V™ has areas that are initially flagged as anomalies. Upon closer examination, many of these areas are due to the fact that the classes are mature classes within a framework. Examples are the *Collection* and *Stream* classes. Overall,

Smalltalk/V does fairly well based on the set of metrics collected.

Number of methods overridden

Smalltalk/V has more than a typical amount of method overrides. This is somewhat due to the number of frameworks built into the image for views and collections.

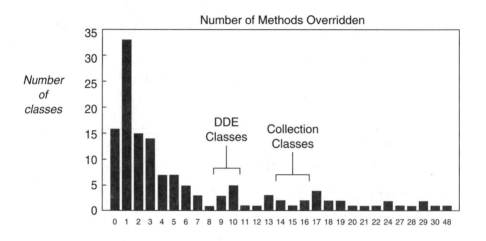

Class hierarchy nesting level

Given the number of frameworks, the nesting is shallower than would be expected. Four to six levels of subclassing are typical, below any framework classes.

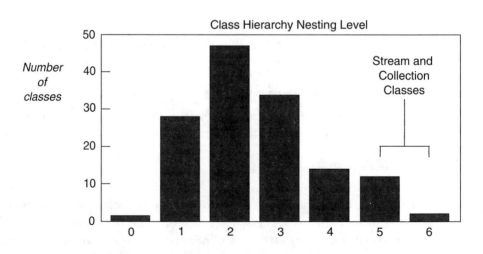

Global usage

Less is better. The larger numbers of global references here are anomalies worth looking into.

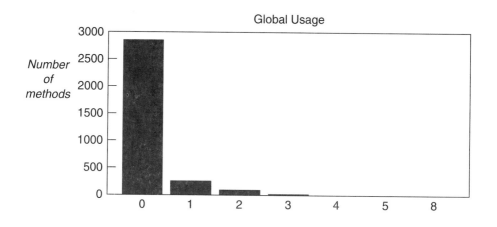

Number of class methods

There are larger numbers of class methods in many classes. Some are certainly understandable, such as for the general-purpose *Date* class. Some class methods are possibly due to the classes being more mature. I would still verify why this many classes have this many class methods.

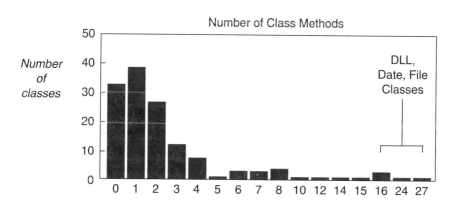

Number of instance variables

The browser class numbers are expected. I'd look into the six-to-nine range to see why this many exist.

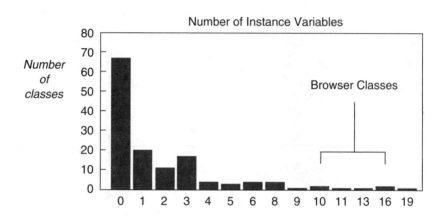

Number of statements

Method sizes look good overall.

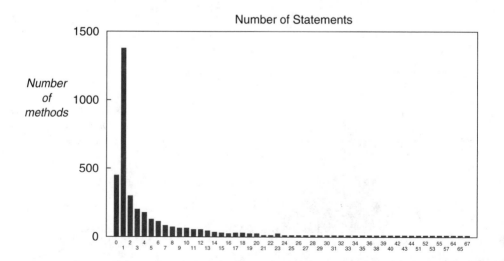

Lines of code

You see some style affects in the histogram pattern, compared to *number of message sends.*

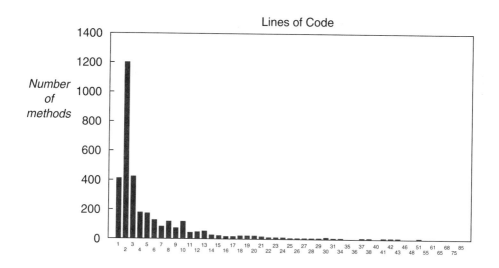

Number of message sends

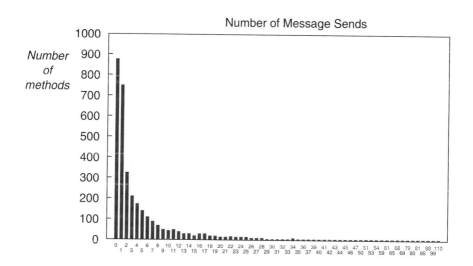

Number of instance methods

General-purpose, mature classes such as the *Stream* and *Collection* classes will have more instance methods.

Lower numbers of instance methods will occur in subclass specializations, which inherit most of their functionality from their superclasses.

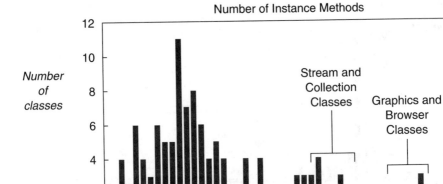

Number of classes

OOMetric has 74 classes and 698 methods.

Project 4—OOMetric™

Type of application

OOMetric™ is an OO metrics analysis tool that measures a number of project and design metrics. It detects anomalies and provides action plans, supports information export to spreadsheets, and works unobtrusively with Smalltalk (and in the future C++) code.

Extent of user interface portion

OOMetric™ has a GUI that includes the use of toolbars, multiple windows, and direct actions via mouse and keyboard.

Length of development effort

Three person-months.

Status

OOMetric™ is in alpha test for Smalltalk code and under development for C++ code.

Development process

Iterative, with the use of beta releases.

Tools used

Smalltalk/V™, WindowBuilder Pro™, HOMSuite™.

Target

Windows™ and OS/2™.

Target language

Smalltalk.

Secondary language

None.

Requirements that necessitated secondary language

Not applicable.

Code product packaging

EXE and DLLs files.

Source of metrics numbers

OOMetric™ from Hatteras Software was used to collect the metrics for itself, of course!

Metric results

OOMetric™ uses many model and UI frameworks. As such, you will see some affects in the metric results.

Number of methods overridden

This application has multiple model and view frameworks, resulting in a number of method overrides by design. The average number of method overrides per class is 2.48. Frameworks drove the numbers higher than would have been the case otherwise. The higher numbers are the result of *better* and not worse design—an indication that blindly enforcing thresholds will not work well.

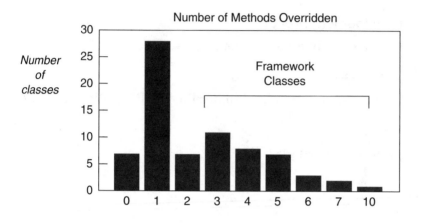

Class hierarchy nesting level

This histogram is characteristic of projects that effectively utilize frameworks. Projects that do not leverage frameworks will have their large jump at the first level of nesting. Multiple frameworks will have multiple jumps in numbers at each of the levels of the framework nestings.

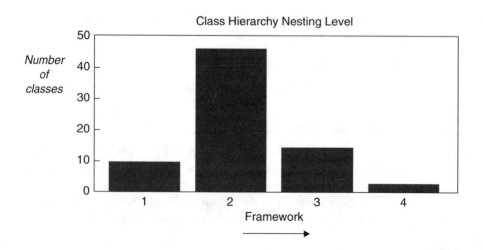

Global usage

Well-designed OO software does not, in general, need very many references to system globals. One global for a "system" object, with a few references, is typically all that's needed.

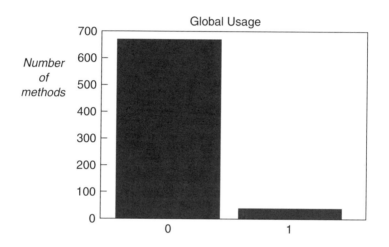

Number of class methods

A number of classes in this system have class methods to return the name of the metrics they collect, thus the high bar for 1.

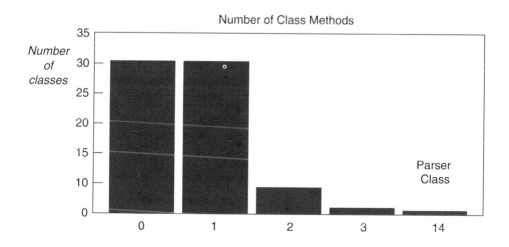

Number of instance variables

The most common classes with higher numbers of instance variables are UI classes. The next most common cases are key classes, central to the application. You would expect key classes to have higher numbers of instance variables, since they are probably junction points of object relationships.

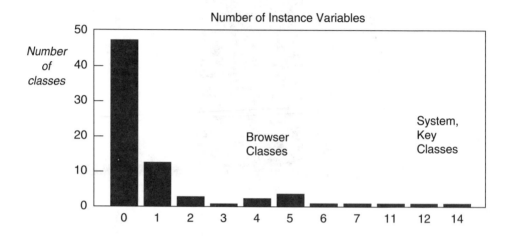

Number of statements

The typical view creation methods are at the top of the numbers. The other cases for this application are the truly self-documenting methods (document generation) and advice generation methods.

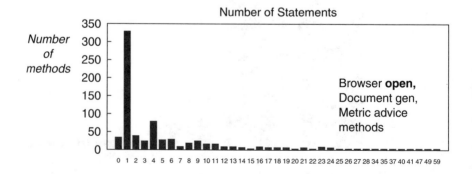

Lines of code

The similar pattern with the *number of message sends* metric indicates that the developers' style did not, in this case, affect the counts much.

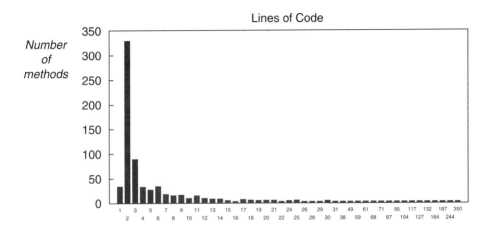

Number of message sends

Again, this is the pattern you should see in your message send counts—a rapid drop in numbers. The average number of message sends per method is 6.55.

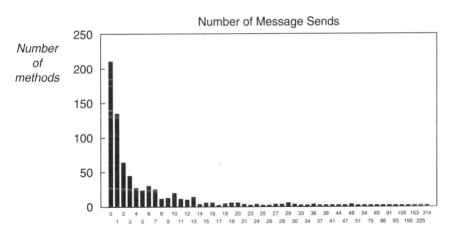

Number of instance methods

Browser classes are to be expected at the higher end of these numbers, since this application has a GUI. The key classes ap-

pear here due to their central focus in the application. They
play a key role in the workings of the application (hence, their
name). I would not worry about the larger numbers for a few
key classes. You will also often see the numbers creep up for
mature classes. The average number of instance methods per
class is 10.18.

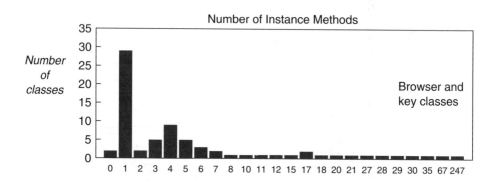

Project 5—Point of Sale Retail

Type of application

The application is a highly interactive fast food sales system.
It focuses on ease of use and supports restaurant sales and
production, including pizza portions and inventory depletion.

Extent of user interface portion

The application has a touch screen GUI.

Length of development effort

Two person-months. This means that an average of approximately 1 person-day was needed per class. The lower number
is largely attributable to the fact that the system is not yet in
production and does not include testing or documentation.

Status

The system is iterating in a prototypical stage of development.

Development process

Multiple iterations. A solid period of object modeling, followed
by cycling between periods of modeling and prototyping.

Tools used

Smalltalk/V™ OS2 for the logic, WindowBuilder Pro™ for the GUI, HOMSuite™ for the analysis and design.

Target

OS/2™.

Target language

Smalltalk/V™ OS2 for the prototype, C++ for the production code.

Code product packaging

To be defined.

Source of metrics numbers

OOMetric™ from Hatteras Software was used to collect the metrics for this product.

Metric results

This application is skewed due to the fact that it is being initially developed in Smalltalk with the intention that it will be adapted to an existing object model built in C++ when it is put into production.

Number of methods overridden

There were some UI and model frameworks used, resulting in a relatively large number of classes with two or three method overrides. The average is 1.57 methods overridden per class.

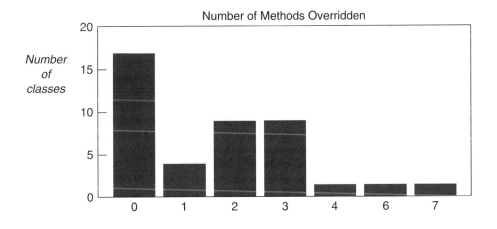

Class hierarchy nesting level

The large number of classes subclassed directly under *Object* is somewhat due to the fact that the class definitions were generated directly from the analysis tool. More focus on framework classes is worth spending time on in this case.

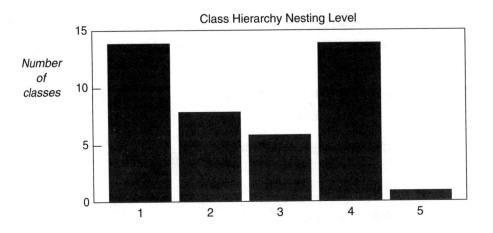

Global usage

A single system global is used.

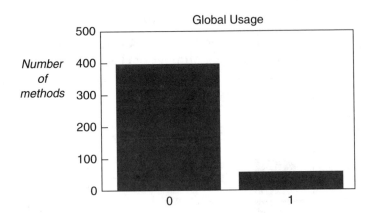

Number of class methods

One class was used to "stock" the inventory with items via class methods. These sets of testbed class methods are responsible for the anomaly in the histogram. Removing this class from the average results in less than 1.5 class methods per class—and that includes the fact that many classes have *class-Comment* class methods generated by the analysis tool.

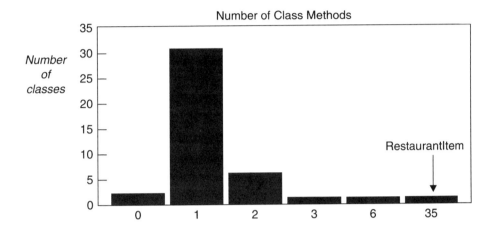

Number of instance variables

A *RestaurantItem* is a key domain class. It is responsible for managing condiments and participating in inventory management. Key classes often end up with higher numbers of instance variables. In this case, the number is high enough that it is worth a look to see if a better design is possibly called for. The average is 1.86 instance variables per class.

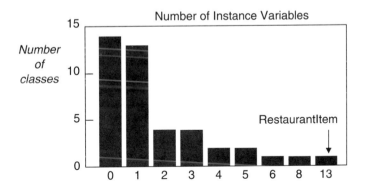

Number of statements

The number of statements don't drop off as dramatically as we would ideally like to see. The duplicate handling of numeric keypad operations across a number of dialog classes needs to be pulled into a common abstract class.

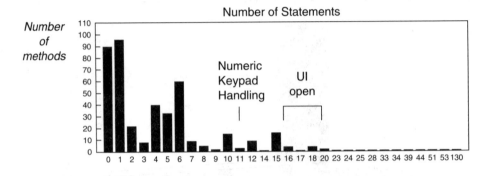

Lines of code

We see some style effects in the different look of the histogram.

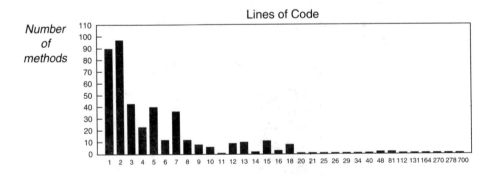

Number of message sends

Most of the higher numbers are due to UI open methods. There are a few methods that handle complex actions, such as separate checks, that may be able to use more delegation and reuse private methods to get their size down. The average is 8.28 messages per method.

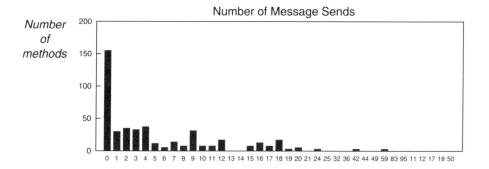

Number of instance methods

All but one of the classes with high numbers of instance methods are GUI classes, as we would expect. The one is *RestaurantSalesLineItem,* which handles all the complexities of special orders from the customer. Again, it is a key class in this domain taking on relatively more responsibilities. The average is 7.78 instance methods per class.

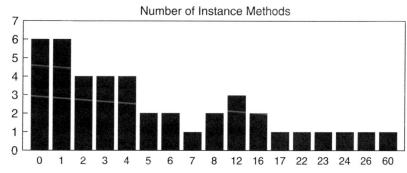

Method complexity

Most of the more complex methods are GUI open methods, to handle the various controls. A couple of other UI methods that fall in the high range are managing the receipt and pushbutton states during the sale.

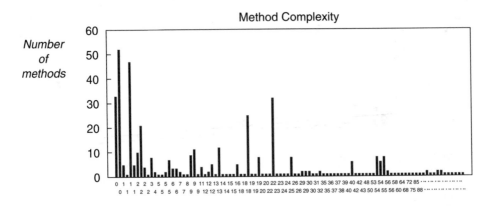

Number of commented methods

After taking an automatically created comment with the developer's initials and date into account as well as the fact that accessing methods don't generally need commentary, the vast majority of the methods have a descriptive comment.

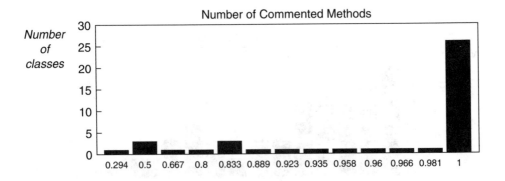

Number of class variables

The average is a low 0.12 class variables per class.

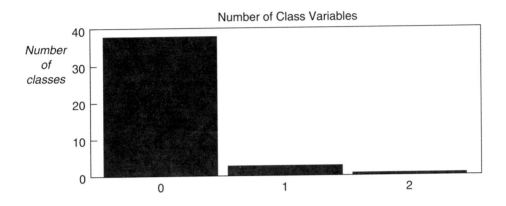

Number of method parameters

Most of the classes with higher averages of method parameters across their methods are UI classes. Users of WindowBuilder Pro™ have noticed that the product generates methods that include the pane as a parameter, whether it's needed or not. This is fine but tends to run the numbers up for this metric.

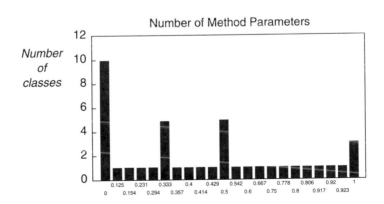

Metrics Form ————————————————————

The following form can be used to collect metrics information from projects. In my experience, the only realistic way to collect information is by using a tool (see the next section). This is because

- no one is likely to collect the information by hand, especially multiple times.

- numbers collected by people instead of tools are biased by the person's interpretation of what is being collected.

Softcopies of the forms can be obtained from the authors.

<Project name> metrics form

Type of application

Enter a description of your project, including the domain (banking, insurance, CAD/CAM, and so on), real time/batch, and other factors that you would deem significant.

Extent of user interface portion

Indicate the complexity of the user interface portion of the project, as related to the rest of the project, such as "significant GUI drag and drop interface which amounted to a relatively large part of the work on the project" or "relatively simple command interface which was not a significant part of the application."

Length of development effort

year(s),   month(s)

Status

Enter the current status of the project, such as "first product released," second release being worked on," "first release in beta test," or "50% complete on first release."

Development process

Enter "Iterative," "Incremental," "Waterfall," or some other name plus a description of what that process is in your organization.

Tools used

Enter a categorized (by phase and types of users) list of tools used on the project.

Target

Enter the platform you are/will run the application on, including the hardware and software.

Target language

Enter the language primarily/solely used to code the application.

Secondary language

Enter any other languages used for the application code.

Requirements that necessitated secondary language

Enter a description of the requirements that necessitated the use of the secondary language.

Code product packaging

Enter information such as "object code only," or "source included for reusable class portions," and/or "dynamic link library."

Source of metrics numbers

Enter information about the tool(s) or methods used to collect the numbers in this form.

Totals

#Application classes	#Modified base classes	Lines of code	Statements	Comment lines	Person-months	#Major iterations

Averages

#LOC per method	#Methods per class (model/UI)	#Instance variables per class	#Person-days per class	#Classes per developer	#Problem reports per class	#Major iterations per class

Sizes

Deepest hierarchy nesting	#Key classes	#Support classes	#Classes thrown away	#Methods thrown away

Team

#Developers	#Testers	#Information developers	#Human factors	#Admin- istrators

Percent person-days per phase

Analysis	Design	Coding	Testing	Documentation

Percentage of classes

New/ modified	Abstract/ concrete

Comments

Enter any comments not covered above that are significant in looking at the project metrics.

Metrics Tools ————————————————————

 In order to have consistency in the statistics you collect, you should use a tool that is based on accepted metric standards. Also, if you are to have any chance at being able to collect the numbers (or motivating people to do so), you need a tool.

Unfortunately, there are not many tools to collect the types of metrics in this book. Most tools the industry has to offer at the time I am writing this book are based on lines of code. As I've explained, this is a poor measurement to base our metrics on.

Some of my tool requirements are

1. Collect OO-specific metrics.

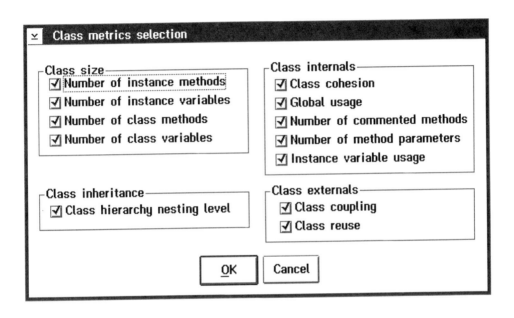

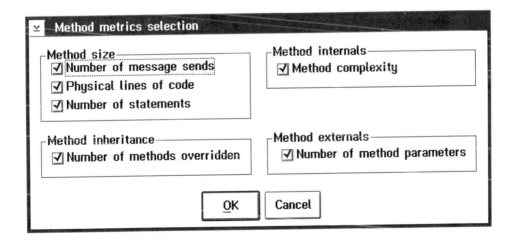

2. Allow user tailoring of thresholds.

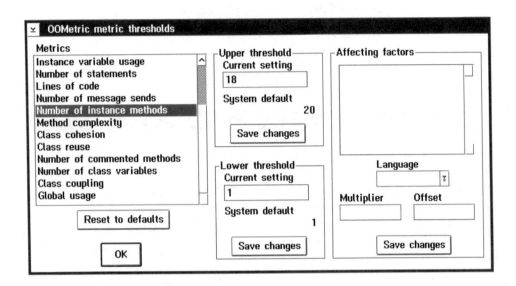

3. Import from and export to industry-standard formats.

4. Touch the system being examined as little as possible. This could be done via DDE queries on Smalltalk images, for example, or parsing C++ files.

5. Filter results and allow searching to find anomalies easily.

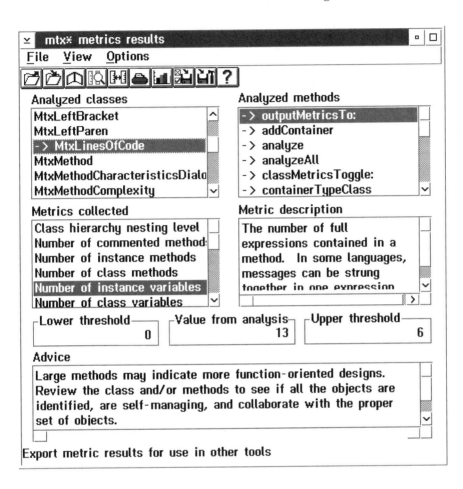

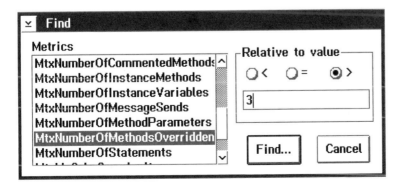

In collecting the metrics detailed in this book, I created (and iterated on) an OO metrics tool (as shown by the screens in this section taken from the alpha version of the tool). Information about this tool, named OOMetric™, for Smalltalk and C++, as well as interpretation of the results of a software metrics analysis, can be obtained from:

Hatteras Software, Inc.
919.851.0993
71214.3120@compuserve.com

Futures

There are a number of areas I would have liked to pursue further for this book, but there comes a time when you have to stop, take the time to document what you've discovered to share with others, and then go on with further efforts. I've listed some areas of interest to me that I have not spent much time on yet.

In addition to these metrics, I'd like to collect metric measurements over time on individual projects to see trends in their values.

Number of scripts per requirement

There should be a relationship between the requirement statements and the number of scripts, test cases, and public methods in the resulting system.

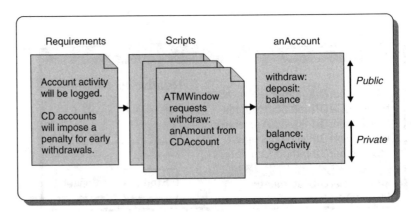

We can use early development process assets, such as requirements and scenario scripts, to develop better estimates early in the effort.

Number of test cases per public method

Relating the number of test cases to the number of public methods, especially contract methods, will help us predict more accurately the amount of effort required to develop a system.

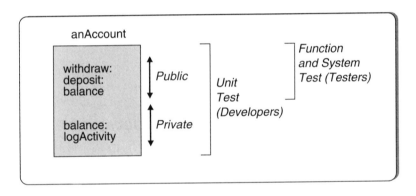

The test cases, preferably derived from the scenario scripts, are run against the public methods by the test organization. By understanding early in the effort how many public interfaces there are in the system, we can predict the level of testing effort facing us.

Runtime metrics

There is certainly a need to collect performance statistics for your system. There are tools out there that can measure execution times. Some of these capabilities come with an OO system, such as those from the Smalltalk vendors, and some are separate products, such as Profile/V™.

Number of class-to-class relationships

The number of classes a class interfaces to affects the amount of coupling. If the classes are in another subsystem, these mes-

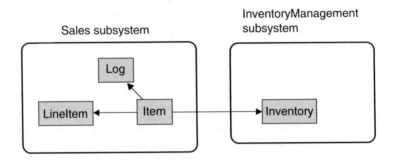

sages affect subsystem coupling.

Number of subsystem-to-subsystem relationships

There should be relatively low message traffic between sub-systems, since they are defined as more tightly coupled class groupings. The classes in a subsystem provide some set of

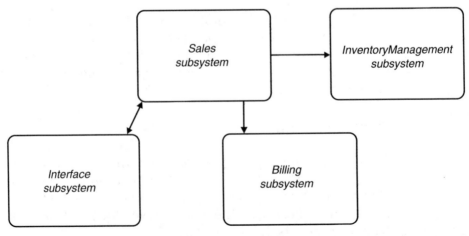

end-user functionality, satisfying one or more contracts.

References

1. Baker, Mark D., "Implementing an initial software metrics program," *IEEE Proceedings of the National Aerospace and Electronics Conference,* vol. 3, 1991, pp. 1289–94.

2. Barnes, G. Michael and Bradley R. Swim, "Inheriting software metrics," *Journal of Object-Oriented Programming,* November/December 1993, pp. 27–34.

3. Boehm, Barry W., "A spiral model of software development and enhancement," *Computer,* vol. 21, no. 5, May 1988, p. 61.

4. Booch, Grady, *Object-Oriented Design with Applications,* Benjamin Cummings Publishing Co., Redwood City, CA, 1991.

5. Bouldin, Barbara M., "What are you measuring? Why are you measuring it?" *Software Magazine,* vol. 9, no. 10, August 1989, pp. 30–39.

6. Boyd, Nik, "Building object-oriented frameworks," *The Smalltalk Report,* vol. 3, no. 1, September 1993, pp. 1–6, 14–16.

7. Card, David N. and Robert L. Glass, *Measuring Software Design Quality,* Prentice Hall, Englewood Cliffs, NJ, 1990.

8. Chidamber, Shyam R. and Chris F. Kemerer, "Towards a metrics suite for object oriented design," *OOPSLA '91 Conference Proceedings,* October 1991, pp. 197–211.

9. Christian, Kaare, "Making exceptions with C++," *PC Magazine,* vol. 12, no. 22, December 21, 1993, pp. 311–20.

10. Dale, C. and Han Van der Zee, "Software productivity metrics–who needs them?" *Eurometrics '92 Proceedings,* April 1992, pp. 31–43.

11. Daskalantonakis, Michael K., "A practical view of software measurement and implementation experiences within Motorola," *IEEE Transactions on Software Engineering,* vol. 18, no. 11, November 1992, pp. 998–1010.

12. DeMarco, T., *Controlling Software Projects*, Prentice Hall, Englewood Cliffs, NJ, 1982.

13. DeVries, Peter, "IBM object oriented metrics," December 1992.

14. Digitalk Inc., *Smalltalk/VPM Tutorial and Programming Handbook*, Digitalk Inc., Los Angeles, CA, 1989.

15. Dreger, J. Brian, *Function Point Analysis*, Prentice Hall, Englewood Cliffs, NJ, 1989.

16. Gibson, Elizabeth, "Objects–born and bred," *Byte Magazine*, October 1990, pp. 245–54.

17. Gilb, T., "Tools for design by objectives," in *Software Requirements Specification and Testing*, Blackwell Scientific Publications, 1985.

18. Goodman, P., "Implementing software metrics programmes: A project-based approach," *Eurometrics '92 Proceedings*, April 1992, pp. 147–51.

19. Grady, Robert B., *Practical Software Metrics for Project Management and Process Improvement*, Prentice Hall, Englewood Cliffs, NJ, 1992.

20. Grady, Robert B. and Deborah L. Caswell, *Software Metrics: Establishing a Company-Wide Program*, Prentice Hall, Englewood Cliffs, NJ, 1987.

21. Henderson-Sellers, B., *A Book of Object-Oriented Knowledge*, Prentice Hall, Englewood Cliffs, NJ, 1992.

22. Henderson-Sellers, B., "Modularization and McCabe's cyclomatic complexity," *Communications of the ACM*, vol. 35, no. 12, December 1992, pp. 17–19.

23. Hinkle, Bob and Ralph Johnson, "Taking exception to Smalltalk," *The Smalltalk Report*, vol. 2, nos. 3 & 4, 1992–1993.

24. Jacobson, Ivar, *Object-Oriented Software Engineering: A Use Case Driven Approach*, Addison-Wesley Publishing Co., Reading, MA, 1992.

25. Jenson, R. and J. Bartley, "Parametric estimation of programming effort: An object-oriented model," *Journal of Systems and Software*, vol. 15, 1991, pp. 107–14.

26. Jones, Capers, *Applied Software Measurement*, McGraw-Hill Publishing, NewYork, 1991.

27. Kemerer, C. F. and B. S. Porter, "Improving the reliability of function point measurement: An empirical study," *IEEE*

Transactions on Software Engineering, vol. 18, no. 11, November 1992, pp. 1011–24.

28. Keyes, Jessica, "New metrics needed for new generation," *Software Magazine,* vol. 12, no. 6, May 1992, pp. 42–56.

29. Kitchenham, B. A., *Managing Complexity in Software Engineering,* National Computer Centre, Manchester, UK, 1990.

30. Kolewe, Ralph, "Metrics in object-oriented design and programming," *Software Development,* vol. 1, no. 4, October 1993, pp. 53–62.

31. Laranjeira, L., "Software size estimation of object-oriented systems," *IEEE Transactions on Software Engineering,* vol. 16, no. 5, May 1990, pp. 510–22.

32. Lorenz, Mark, *Object-Oriented Software Development: A Practical Guide,* Prentice Hall, Englewood Cliffs, NJ, 1993.

33. Lorenz, Mark, "Real world reuse," *Journal of Object-Oriented Programming,* November/December 1991, pp. 35–39.

34. McCabe, T. J., "A complexity measure," *IEEE Transactions on Software Engineering,* vol. 2, 1976, pp. 308–20.

35. Meyers, Scott, *Effective C++,* Addison-Wesley Publishing Co., Reading, MA, 1992.

36. Putnam, Larry and Ware Myers, *Measures for Excellence: Reliable Software on Time, Within Budget,* Yourdon Press/Prentice Hall, Englewood Cliffs, NJ, 1992.

37. Rains, E., "Function points in an Ada object-oriented design?" *OOPS Messenger,* vol. 2, no. 4, October 1991, pp. 23–25.

38. Sakkinen, M., "Disciplined inheritance," *Proceedings of the 1989 European Conference on Object Oriented Programming (ECOOP),* pp. 39–56.

39. Stroustrup, Bjarne, *The C++ Programming Language,* Addison-Wesley Publishing Co., Reading, MA, 1987.

40. West, Martin, "An investigation of C++ metrics to improve C++ project estimation," IBM internal paper dated October 12, 1992.

41. Wild, Frederic H. III, "Managing class coupling," *Unix Review,* vol. 9, no. 10, October 1991, pp. 45–47.

42. Wirfs-Brock, Rebecca et al., *Designing Object-Oriented Software,* Prentice Hall, Englewood Cliffs, NJ, 1990.

43. Yourdon, Edward, *Object-Oriented Systems Design,* Yourdon Press/Prentice Hall, Englewood Cliffs, NJ, 1994.

44. "The Deming Prize: No longer a stranger at home," *Computerworld,* vol. 23, no. 50, December 11, 1989, p. 100.

Glossary

Abstract class

A class which has no instances. A class which contains common methods and state data to facilitate sharing among its subclasses.

Accessing method

A method which is used to *get* or *set* an instance variable. Accessing methods allow you to perform laissez-faire initialization. They are usually very short, almost standard, methods that are left out of some measurements.

Analysis

That part of software development concerned with modeling a (part of a) business.

Anomaly

A deviation from the common result.

Application completion metric

A metric that deals with the dynamic characteristics of a project, such as *number of contracts completed.*

Class

A template that defines the structure and capabilities of an object instance. The class definition includes the state data and the behaviors for the instances of that class.

Class hierarchy

A tree structure that organizes class inheritance.

Class hierarchy nesting

The number of subclassing levels from the top in the class hierarchy.

Comment line

A physical line in a method or class definition that contains a comment.

Concrete class

A class with instances in the runtime system.

Contract

A simplifying abstraction of a group of related public responsibilities that are to be provided by subsystems and classes to their clients.

Design

That part of software development concerned with the mapping of a business model into an implementation.

Design metric

A metric that deals with the static characteristics of a project, such as *number of methods in a class*.

Framework

A set of prebuilt classes and methods that define the basic structure of some end-user functions, leaving the application-specific details to be filled in by developers.

Heuristic

A guideline based on trial-and-error usage. A rule of thumb.

Incremental process

Development steps that result in piecemeal additions of new application functions over the life of the project.

Instance variable

A name that allows one object (instance) to refer to another one. The instance variables make up an object's state data.

Iteration

A single cycle of an iterative process, consisting of *planning, production,* and *assessment* phases over a multimonth period of time.

Iterative process

Development steps that result in multiple deliveries of the same application functions over the life of the project.

Key class

A class that is central to the business domain being automated. A key class is one that would cause great difficulties in developing and maintaining a system if it did not exist.

Laissez-faire initialization

A technique whereby instance variables are initialized when they are needed and not beforehand. This allows for more self-managing objects and system robustness, with a cost in additional overhead.

Line item

A unit of effort on a software project, assigned to one person and developed during one iteration.

LOC

Line of code. A measurement that has traditionally been used as the primary estimation and progress indicator on software projects, with poor results.

Measurement

The determination of the value of a metric for a particular object.

Method size

A measure of the volume of a method, based on attributes such as number of message sends and types of message sends.

Method

A class service or behavior. Methods are executed whenever an object receives a message. They contain the logic, in the form of more message sends, for the objects in a class.

Method complexity

A measure of the amount of work and number of decisions being made by a method, which has development and maintenance implications.

Method override

To create a method in a class with the same name as a method in one of its superclasses. This results in different behavior for the same message.

Metric

A standard of measurement. Used to judge the attributes of something being measured, such as quality or complexity, in an unbiased manner.

OO

Object-oriented.

Reuse

To use something in a new situation without modification (black box). To use something in a new situation with modification (white box).

Scenario script

A sequence of steps the user and system take to accomplish some task. There is a script for each of the major end-user functions provided by the system.

Specialization

An extension of the behavior of a type of object.

Subsystem

A group of classes that work together to provide a related group of end-user functions.

Support class

A class that is not central to the business domain being automated but provides basic services or interface capabilities to the key classes.

Threshold value

A measurement value that has been determined through project experiences to be significant in terms of desirable or undesirable designs, with some margin of error. Generally, these will be tunable over time as you gain experiences specific to your business and teams.

Use case

See *Scenario script*.

Index